God Rules

God Rules

The Commandments, the Beatitudes, and the Virtues for Teens and Young Adults

By

L. A. Carstens

Based on the series originally published in *Veritas/YOU*
Catholic Youth Magazine

ISBN: 978-0-557-09089-1

Based on the series originally published in Veritas/YOU

Catholic Youth Magazine

For Rebecca, James, Sarah, John, and Catherine: I began work on this in the sunset of my youth; may it guide and inspire you as the dawn rises on yours. Read it; resist the world, the flesh, and the devil; and find unending joy and fulfillment in the living God.

"You are young and you are the future/ So suck it up and tough it out and be the best you can"

--John Cougar Mellencamp

Acknowledgments

There are always many people to be thanked whenever a book, even a little one like this, is written. Since this book's purpose is to help readers learn about right and wrong, I would like to acknowledge those who taught me to choose what is right and good from my childhood. I will always be thankful to my own parents, who met my bodily needs by providing food, clothing, and shelter and met my spiritual needs by being decent, ethical people. Then there are all the teachers who taught me important things—some taught me about the Catholic faith, others taught me about morality in general, and others (even if they were not Catholics) exposed me to the many aspects of truth.

Those I would thank by name are: Mrs. Poole, my memorable second grade teacher in the Parents' Cooperative School in Jeddah, Saudi Arabia (where I received my First Communion at the American Consulate in 1971); my sixth grade teacher, Sr. Mary Rose, CSJ; my spiritual director in St. Vincent's Minor (high school) Seminary, Fr. (and now Dr.) David E. Windsor, CM; and two college professors named James who were both marked with the sign of faith, Mr. James Antonioli and Dr. James Hanink, who taught me English and philosophy, respectively—more importantly, they taught me about life, character, and faith in God. Other priests who have been good friends and wise guides (as opposed to wiseguys) are Fr. Alexei Smith, Fr. Rene Shatteman, and Fr. Vaughn Winters.

I must also thank my past editors: Donna Thompson, who first encouraged me to write for the school paper of Loyola Marymount University in 1988, and Paul Lauer, who deserves the credit for the idea of this series. As editor for *Veritas* (later *YOU!*) *Magazine*, he first asked me to write these essays for the magazine in the early 1990s. I also owe a debt of gratitude to Dale Vree, who published a number of my letters and essays in *The New Oxford Review*. I've had my disagreements with Dale, but that takes nothing away from my debt to him as an editor who encouraged and helped me with the craft of writing.

As for the creative imagery in the book, there may be some debts I have forgotten to acknowledge, but not on purpose. The ones I can bring to mind now appear in one of the more wacky of the installments: Beatitude #6 ("Blessed are the pure in heart"). The name of the alien was borrowed from Tom Ehart, managing editor of *YOU! Magazine* at the time. Some of the imagery for the alien was inspired by the hilarious novel *The Hitchhiker's Guide to the Galaxy*, by Douglas Adams (a very funny and gifted author, though, of course, I don't agree with his atheism.) Some elements of the characters in the humorous high school scenes were borrowed from the teen comedies of John Hughes (*Sixteen Candles*, for sure, and possibly others).

There are certain Web sites that deserve mention since they provided important references as these essays were being crafted and revised: www.catholic.com, the Web site of Catholic Answers, and the Catholic Encyclopedia at www.newadvent.org. Also, the U.S. Conference of Catholic Bishops has an excellent Web site that provides handy online access to the Catechism of the Catholic Church (www.usccb.org/catechism/text), which was a great help.

Of course, I cannot fail to mention my debt to the Ignatius Bible, the one modern English Catholic version of the Bible I trust the most, since it suffers from none of the politically correct follies and feminizations so common in other modern translations. All of the direct quotes from scripture in this book are from the Ignatius Bible. Even when using a quote from another source, I consulted that trusty, blue/gold covered book to check the exact wording and make sure it was just right.

I am indebted to a number of authors who are quoted within the text, but since they are mentioned in the last section (Recommendations for Further Reading) I will not repeat them here.

And as married authors often do, I would like to thank my wife, Mary Ann, and our five precious children for all their sacrifices of my time and attention when I was working on this project, which now spans eighteen years. I also thank Mary Ann's extended family, my extended family, all of our dear friends, and my colleagues and students at Francis Polytechnic High School and College of the Canyons. Each of you has taught me and enriched my life, whether you realized it or not, through your friendship, your humor, and, yes, even your criticism.

Larry A. Carstens

Castaic, CA (a suburb of the City of Our Lady, Queen of Los Angeles)

Summer, 2008

Preface

Welcome to *God Rules*. This is the kind of little book that sometimes gets given as a gift because someone in your life thought it might do you some good. If you're actually reading it, that's step in the right direction. Now, let's see how far you get …

A popular trend in today's society shows up in the common advertising slogan, "no rules." Similar phrases are "no boundaries" or "without limits." Variations on this theme are seen not only in advertising, but in popular books, magazines, TV shows, movies, and political rhetoric. When people fight for something they know in their hearts is wrong, they call it "a right to choose" and say, "Don't impose your morality on me!" Today's typical secular humanist college professor constantly drums it into his students' heads that there is no absolute right or wrong and morality is just a human invention created by dead white males to oppress women and people of color. (The next time a teacher or professor tells you there is no absolute right or wrong, ask him if it would be *absolutely wrong* to say there *are* things that are absolutely right or wrong.) Right off the bat, merely talking about rules, morality, or right and wrong is to be countercultural in today's world. But when Pope John Paul II came to visit the United States, he actually used that term: "Do not be afraid to be countercultural for Christ's sake." Even George Washington, recognizing the trends of his day (the anti-God currents of the Endarkenment—oops, I mean Enlightenment), said, "Reason and experience forbid us to expect that national morality can prevail in exclusion of religious principle." So even if popular culture and professional lawsuit filers like the ACLU do all they can to lead us in the opposite direction, the best and brightest have long recognized the need for morality, ethics, and right and wrong—the rules of God, by any other name.

In contrast with the prevailing views of popular culture, author C. S. Lewis pointed out (in his book *Mere Christianity*) that rules are not the enemy of freedom but the very things that make true freedom possible. It is only because there are rules of the road that drivers have the freedom to go to destinations of their choosing. If nobody stopped at red lights or drove on the right side of the road, it would be impossible to get anywhere in a car. If you really think about it, rules are not the enemy of freedom, but the prerequisite for it. The "no rules" mentality is actually a recipe not for freedom, but for a type of slavery: enslavement to one's desires. "No rules" is a common advertising slogan because the advertising industry attempts to influence people to blindly pursue their desires, thereby driving profits. If you fall under the influence of the "no rules" slogan, instead of bothering about old-fashioned ideas of right and wrong, you'll just buy whatever seems new, hip, and flashy without thinking about what you're doing, which is what the "no rules" spin doctors want you to do. Someone who is a slave to his desires is not likely to stop and think about whether or not he should buy something. Or, as they say, a fool and his money are soon parted. (Or was that a fool and his money are soon partying? Probably the same difference anyway ...)

The Church has always been in the unique position of defying the prevailing culture and holding firm to what is true and righteous. There are many examples of this in the Church's history (for a full exploration of this topic, check out Harry W. Crocker's Triumph: The Power and the Glory of the Catholic Church). During the barbarian onslaught of the Dark Ages, the Church was the only institution in Europe that preserved the learning and culture of ancient Greece and Rome. Without it, there would have been no Renaissance. During the 1930s, the Church was the only institution in Germany that stood up to Adolf Hitler. Even though a lot of secular historians prefer to ignore these facts (especially how Pope Pius XII saved hundreds of thousands of Jews), the great German Jewish scientist Albert Einstein wrote, "Being a lover of freedom, when the [Nazi] revolution came in Germany, I looked to the universities to defend it, knowing they had always boasted of their devotion to the cause of truth; but no, the universities were silenced. Then I looked to the great editors of newspapers whose flaming editorials in days gone by had proclaimed their love of freedom; but they, like the universities, were silenced in a few short weeks ... Only the Church stood squarely across the path of Hitler's campaign for suppressing truth. I never had any special interest in the Church before, but now I feel a great affection and admiration because the Church alone has had the courage and persistence to stand for intellectual truth and moral freedom. I am forced thus to confess that what I once despised I now praise unreservedly." (Time, December 23, 1940). Even Einstein didn't want to recognize the heroic role the

Church had played, but because he was an honest and principled guy (not to mention extremely intelligent—you don't have to be Einstein to figure that out!), he did. Far more often than most people realize, the Church has played a positive role in its defiance of popular culture.

And that is still the role of the Church today. At a time when almost all the powerful, influential, and beautiful people agree that rules, morality, and anything connected to organized religion are out, the Church is still there to say: "Whoa!" and "Check yourself before you wreck yourself!" (Maybe not in those words exactly, but you get the idea...) A number of media commentators have expressed amazement at the constant popularity of the Pope among young people (at the time they were talking about Pope John Paul II, but it also applies to the current pontiff, Benedict XVI). His popularity among the young was constant "in spite of" his strong and uncompromising stand in regard to Church teaching and traditional morality. These commentators never understood that it wasn't *in spite of* but *because of* his strong and uncompromising stand on Church teaching and traditional morality that young people were drawn to him. They were growing up in a world where adults were often too scared or wimpy to be adults and demand good behavior from their kids. The result was a widespread thirst among young people for an adult voice that wasn't afraid to be an adult voice, a voice that would take a strong stand about right and wrong and would say so—with love, of course, but without confusion, compromise, or fuzzy thinking. Unlike many teachers, professors, and parents, the Pope never told young people there's no such thing as right and wrong. And the natural thirst of young people for clear concepts of right and wrong was satisfied by his leadership. That thirst can still be satisfied by the teachings of the Church as long as teens and young adults get a chance to learn about them.

It is for this purpose this little book was written. The Commandments, Beatitudes, and Virtues don't get much coverage nowadays, and the number of young people who could name all of them is slim. As for the number who could actually explain what each of them means, it is probably even smaller. Hopefully, this collection of essays may change that. The God Rules are worth knowing and worth living. Reading this will help with the knowing part—the rest is up to you.

xii

The phrase "God Rules" sounds like a cool way teens and young adults might describe the awesome power of our Heavenly Father. Well, it's also a way to summarize and describe three sets of rules that come from God and that can help us find our way to him. The Commandments, the Beatitudes, and the Virtues can be called the God Rules because they provide directions for how to live as we are meant to live. When you buy almost any product, what is the first thing you (at least *should*) pull out? The directions! Any even slightly complicated product comes with instructions from the manufacturer on proper use. In the same way, the Manufacturer whose product we are has included a set of instructions for the proper care and usage of his products. Some people completely ignore the instructions and then wonder why their lives get broken so quickly. Others read them half way and then sort of follow some of them sometimes, but not other times. Then they end up using the product the wrong way and having to pay for costly repairs. And, finally, there are others who read the instructions all the way through and follow them carefully. These are the ones whose product lasts the longest and gives them the most joy and satisfaction.

If you read these instructions and follow them carefully and attentively for the rest of your days, the Manufacturer has guaranteed a long and happy life (of course, the longest and happiest part happens after earthly life passes away). What happens when you break the rules? Part of the whole setup is the understanding that this Manufacturer is all about love and forgiveness. "Have I any pleasure in the death of the wicked, says the Lord God, and not rather that he should turn from his way and live?" (Ezek. 18:23). Christ also stated, "I came not to call the righteous, but sinners" (Matt. 9:13). If you haven't followed all the rules perfectly, here's a little secret: *Nobody* has obeyed them perfectly for about the last two thousand years. But as author Robert Louis Stevenson once wrote, "The saints are the sinners who keep on trying." As long as we're on this earth we are a work in progress, and having a clear understanding of God's rules is not meant to oppress us or scare us, but to help us to become the free, strong, and happy people God created us to be.

One last issue should be addressed here. We already covered the objections people might have to rules, morality, or anything that says there are moral absolutes. One more objection may remain: there are those who say, "Learning about religion or rules sounds boring!" What can be said in response? How about this: don't judge a book by its cover. If you actually read the essays in this collection, you'll probably see they're anything but boring—a little weird sometimes, a little corny here and there, off the wall, maybe, but not boring. Still have your doubts? Well, there's only one way to find out for sure: turn the page and start reading.

Hope to see you in heaven some day, and hope this little book helps you get there!

L. A. Carstens

Contents

Introduction to the Ten Commandments

What are the Ten Commandments? They are the code of laws that were inscribed on two stone tablets on Mount Sinai and delivered by Moses to the Hebrews not long after God delivered the chosen people from slavery in Egypt. It was as if God said, "Here's your freedom, now use it to follow my laws and freely choose good and avoid evil."

But how did we get to the time of Moses? Here's a brief summary of God's relationship with his chosen people. First, God called Abraham to begin a new people, promising him his descendants would be as numerous as the stars. Abraham's son was Isaac, and Isaac's son was Jacob. Jacob's youngest son was Joseph, whose older brothers betrayed him and threw him down a well. Then what? Well, well, well. Joseph was sold into slavery in Egypt, but as the years went by he became an important and powerful dude there. When a famine hit, his influence on Pharaoh led Pharaoh to invite Joseph's big, extended family to Egypt. Years later, a new Pharaoh took over Egypt and started treating the Hebrews badly, even to the point of enslaving them and killing some of their children. Then Moses came along and, responding to God's call, led the Hebrew people out of Egypt.

Instead of being thankful and loyal to God, the chosen people turned away, grumbled about their hardships, and started worshipping idols. In other words, the people had been freed from slavery in Egypt but now were falling into another form of slavery—enslavement to their desires, doubts, and fears, the kind of slavery people fall into when they reject God. That's when Moses and the Ten Commandments came in. While the Israelites were encamped at Sinai, Moses went up to the mountain and heard God's voice from a burning bush. He received the Ten Commandments on two stone tablets and delivered them to God's chosen people. Just like people today, many of them had turned to idolatry, spiritual laziness, and wickedness. The commandments were given to help them return to God and his ways.

Some people today complain that most of the Ten Commandments start with "Thou shalt not ..." –and this seems negative, oppressive and limiting. The best response to this complaint is that the commandments weren't given to entertain people; they were given to help people be good. Most of them start with commands *not* to do something because ever since Adam and Eve disobeyed God in the Garden of Eden, we humans have tended to do a lot of things we shouldn't. In other words, Moses was given a series of prohibitions because the people of his time needed to stop doing a lot of what they were doing. Nowadays, the commandments still apply because, well, a lot of people of *our* time should stop doing a lot of what they're doing!

The focus did change somewhat when Christ entered the scene— generally there were fewer "thou shalt nots" and more "you shoulds"— and the early Church debated the issue and determined that the Ten Commandments still applied. As Christ said, "Think not I have come to abolish the law and the prophets; I have come not to abolish them but to fulfill them" (Matt. 5:17). God has lovingly revealed himself and his teachings in different ways over the last three thousand years, but some things have remained constant. The Ten Commandments were the first codified set of rules he gave to his people. Later, when he became man, he revealed more about who he was. Then, after Christ's life, death, and resurrection, the Holy Spirit—guiding the Church—continued his work. The teachings have grown, like a tree, but they have not morphed into something completely different. For this reason, the older teachings still apply; the Ten Commandments are still worth knowing and following.

It has pleased God to place a similar sense of morality in every human culture. Even though he revealed himself directly to Moses, he revealed himself indirectly to all people. It's interesting to note that the Ten Commandments are echoed in all cultures and religions. The code of Hammurabi, the Upanishads, the ancient Chinese Tao, and even the traditional tribal codes of the American Indians and Africans—all forbid stealing, dishonesty, and murder of the innocent; and all of them encourage respect for one's parents and, if not God, at least "the gods." (A good illustration of this can be found in the appendix to C. S. Lewis's *The Abolition of Man*.) This shows that God revealed his laws directly in one time and place but indirectly to all people everywhere.

Now it's time for you to learn about the first set of God Rules. Turn the page, and we're off ...

The First Commandment: "Thou Shalt Not Have Other Gods besides Me"

Bottom Line: God should come first in our lives: No false gods should get any air time in our heads. If they do, that makes us airheads.

The host of *America's Screaming Teen Idols* introduced the current crop of contestants to the national audience. "Each one of these people has worked really hard to get here. Which one will be the next Screaming Teen Idol? We'll find out after some words from our sponsors." Several commercials appeared on the screen, each trying to get viewers to buy things they didn't really need. Millions of viewers watched images that increased their desires to own things they would never have, to be with people they would never meet, or to look like people they would never resemble. Some viewers thought about the opposite sex, others thought about what was wrong with their appearance, others thought about food, others thought about making money, and a few thought about changing the channel. How many of them thought about God? If you answered very few or none, you win a prize.

We are surrounded by idols. Even the term *idol* is not something we think of as negative. The actual definition of idol (found in Webster's Dictionary) includes the phrase "a false god." And while it may be harmless as a way of describing a popular celebrity, we have to ask ourselves why it has become such a frequently used term. Could it be that we subconsciously know we worship all kinds of false gods? People sometimes speak of celebrity worship and describe fans as forming a cult following for a show, group, or person because these beautiful people have become objects of pseudo-religious devotion in today's society. Human beings were made to worship God, and when they turn away from him, they end up worshipping something else, even if they don't think of it as worship. A quote often attributed to G. K. Chesterton (though he didn't actually write the exact words) is, "The first effect of not believing in God is to believe in anything." And since so many people in modern society have turned away from God, a lot of things—or people—are being worshipped in his place.

What Is Idolatry?

Idolatry is the worship of anyone or anything other than the living God. And it has a long history. Most of the tribes and peoples that surrounded the ancient Hebrews worshipped idols, but the tribe of Israel brought forth the monotheistic faith: the teaching that there is one God over all. The Israelites themselves sometimes fell into idol worship, such as with the Golden Calf (Exod. 32:8), and had to be brought back to God by Moses and later by the prophets. During the Dark Ages, the pre-Christian pagans of Europe worshipped idols who also called for human sacrifice. In what is now Mexico, the Aztecs worshipped idols that demanded human sacrifice (as did many of the idols of the Old Testament, which means that idols in history often acted more like demons than gods). The Aztecs only stopped their child sacrifices when the apparition of Our Lady of Guadalupe led to mass conversions.

Written during the Renaissance, Shakespeare's play *Romeo and Juliet* portrays two teenagers who idolize each other. Juliet calls Romeo "the god of my idolatry" (Act 2, Scene 2), and the two lovers constantly refer to each other with the language of religious devotion. Shakespeare demonstrates that romantic love can sometimes become a form of idolatry. The play ends in tragedy because no human being can or should be the focus of that kind of devotion (in which you live for the other person). That kind of devotion belongs to God alone, and worshipping another person in that way is another form of idolatry.

In the twentieth century, dictators like Lenin, Stalin, and Hitler promoted another form of idolatry: the state. They hated traditional Judeo-Christian religion and tried to replace it with godless ideologies like communism or Nazism, and for a number of years they got away with it: people in their countries followed and worshipped them as if they were gods. These demonic dictators thanked their people by murdering millions.

So what does it mean nowadays to not have other gods besides God? It's not likely your friends are going to come up to you and say, "Hey, dude, let's go worship in the temple of Baal!" or "Praise the name of Moloch!" But they might try to influence you to participate in another form of idol worship. Even without friends around, spending hours in front of the TV or computer can turn into a form of idolatry. Another form of idolatry today is a sick worship of a twisted concept of freedom (i.e. "pro-choice") that calls for the shedding of innocent human blood in the form of abortion.

Then What's *Not* Idolatry?

If all these things are forms of idolatry, how do we follow this commandment to avoid idolatry? The answer is that you put God first before anything or anyone else. That doesn't mean you can't enjoy listening to music, watching a good film, falling in love, or using a computer. But it does mean you need to be on your guard that none of these things takes so much of your time and attention that you forget God or ignore his calling in your life. Even good things can become idolatry if they erase or gradually steal away our devotion to the living God.

What then is not idolatry? Some non-Catholic Christians use the term *idolatry* to attack Catholics because we pray to the Blessed Mother and the saints, but they are wrong. Catholics do not *worship* the Virgin Mary or the saints any more than you worship a friend if you ask him to pray for you. And if you can ask friends on earth to pray for you, why can't you ask friends in heaven? We honor God by honoring his Mother and asking for her help and intercession. The same is true for saints and angels. The Bible (which was put together by the Catholic Church in the first few centuries AD) directs us to honor God by honoring the saints in heaven (Heb. 12). And the first saint, the Queen of Heaven and Queen of the Angels, is God's Mother, Mary. If anyone tries to tell you that honoring her is a form of idolatry, ask him this: is reading the Bible or listening to a pastor also a form of idolatry? No way, José. We honor God by honoring those he calls us to honor, both on earth and in heaven. That's not idolatry; that's what our obedience to him leads us to do.

Another activity that is not idolatry has to do with statues and images in our churches and homes. Most people keep pictures of people they love. Unless they are crazy, they don't start talking to the pictures and thinking they are the real people. In the same way, statues and images help us in our devotion to God. We're not worshipping them or confusing them with God, so it's also wrong for certain puritanical Christians to claim this is idolatry. Misguided Christians sometimes cite the passage in Exodus (20:3–6) that warns against making "graven images" for purposes of idolatry. But they ignore other parts of the Bible in which God commands making "graven images" for other purposes (Exod. 25:18–19, Num. 21: 8–9, and 1 Kings 6:23, 27–29). For more information on this and similar topics, check out www.catholic.com (the official Web site of Catholic Answers).

The Wrap

So, first things first: the First Commandment means who's on first? Don't say "I dunno!" The correct answer is that God should be first in all things. Even our money says "In God we trust." Not only money, but no fame, fortune, state, or ideology; no girlfriend/boyfriend; or any show, celebrity, or video game should come before God. Thousands of idols have come and gone: they rise up and have their moment in the sun, then bite the dust—but God lives on. The First Commandment means forget the idols and never let anything steal your focus from him. Ditch the false gods; follow the only one true God.

The Second Commandment: "Thou Shalt Not Take the Name of the Lord Thy God in Vain"

Bottom Line: Any time we use any name that refers to God it should respect and glorify him. What's in a name? Plenty. If we don't respect names that refer to God, we're not respecting him.

Gee whiz! Golly! Gosh darn it! What do each of these expressions have in common? They're all corny expressions from old movies and TV shows from the 1950s? Maybe, but what else? Do you notice how each of them starts off sounding similar to words like *Jesus* or *God*? Corny they may be, but they represent expressions that came about from people trying to honor the Second Commandment. They were attempts to avoid saying words that would offend religious people, and they eventually worked their way into everyday vocabulary.

Why would religious people be offended by people using God's name in vain? Could it be because *God* is offended by people using his name in vain? That's the ticket!

What Is the Name of the Lord God?

Unfortunately for those who like to take the easy way out, the answer here is: there are tons of them. *Tons of what?* Tons of names that refer to God. One of the earliest is simply "I am." Then there were others in the Old Testament, like Yahweh, Jehovah, and El-Shaddai. In the New Testament, there is the Word, Jesus Christ, the Father, the Son, and the Holy Spirit. There are many other titles and names for God, including Wonderful Counselor, Son of Righteousness, Son of Man, and Lamb of God. There is also the mighty important formulation found in the Gospel of John, "God is Love."

Can these titles be used in ways that violate the Second Commandment? They can. Or they can be used in ways that do not violate it. It all depends on how you use them.

What Is "In Vain?"

The expression "in vain" refers to something that does not achieve its purpose. For example, the expression "he died in vain" means that someone's death did not achieve its purpose. If a man died trying to save someone else, and that person died, too, people would say he died in vain because his death did not achieve its purpose (though, of course, things may look quite different from the standpoint of heaven …). Someone who works hard and saves a lot of money for a goal, then finds out the goal can't be achieved, might say, "I worked so hard and it was all in vain!"

So what does it mean to take the Lord's name in vain? It means that a person uses words that refer to God in a way that does not achieve their purpose. There are two legitimate ways we can use God's name without violating the commandment: in prayer or in speech that glorifies God or teaches others about him. Even if you are not actually praying, there's nothing wrong with speaking about God—even using his name—in a way that thanks him for the beauty of creation, tells others about him, or wishes his blessings (e.g., "May God bless you.") One way Christianity differs from other world religions has to do with its assertion that God became one of us—he is not just some unreachable, untouchable, far-off cosmic super-force, but he is our brother and friend, "one like us in all things but sin" (Heb. 4:15). And since he chose to call us friends and because friends share what they have, he has chosen to share knowledge of who he is, including his names.

And how have we responded to his sharing? Many of us have not responded very well. How many times have you heard people using names that refer to God out of anger, frustration, or disrespectful mockery? How many times, in the multimillion dollar entertainment industries (movies, TV, cable, satellite, and popular radio), does this happen? The number is not small. But the truth is the truth, and God's law is God's law. "Everybody does it" doesn't count as a valid excuse. Besides, if you look carefully, it's not true that everybody does anything! There are always exceptions, even to the most pervasive trends in popular culture. There are some people who honor this commandment, and if you ask the people in your life who try to seriously live their faith, you'll find out who they are.

Turn a Sin into a Win

If you're like a lot of young people today, there probably are times you have used God's names in vain: without praying and without speaking soberly about God, but instead when you were angry, shocked, or trying to impress someone else. Was it wrong to use God's names like that? You need to answer that for yourself, and hopefully you know a good confessor you can see sometime soon!

If you have fallen into this habit, try to turn it around. The next time you use God's name in vain, keep talking, but in a way that causes the words to achieve their purpose. What does that mean? That means, instead of just throwing around words that refer to God, actually start talking to him, and say something that actually achieves good in his sight. For example, the next time you blurt out, "Oh, God!" or "Jesus," follow it up with "have mercy on me, a sinner" or "thank you for all your gifts" or "help me get through this situation." In that way, something that started out sinful actually becomes good. What would have been a sin becomes a win: instead of using God's names in vain, you will use them for the purpose he gave them to us—to grow closer to him and speak to him as our brother and friend, yet one so holy and sacred that even his names deserve our respect.

The Third Commandment: "Remember to Keep Holy the Lord's Day"

Bottom Line: Sunday is not just another day, business as usual, ho hum.Sunday is a day specially blessed by God. If it ever becomes just like the other six days, something's hurtin' for certain.

Before there was an Internet, hybrid cars, paychecks, homework, bosses or teachers, and everything else in the fast-paced, work-a-day world, there was God. And before everything else got created, God *was*. One of the earliest ways he revealed himself was by saying simply "I am." He didn't say, "And I can do all kinds of amazing stuff!" There are two basic aspects of anyone's existence, whether God's or ours: *being* and *doing*. *Being* has to do with *who you are*. *Doing* has to do with *what you do*. Doing always flows from being. God was God before he created the universe and everything in it. Likewise, a person is a person regardless of his job or accomplishments (even if he can't *do* anything, like someone in a coma or a baby in the womb). God loves us first and foremost because of who we are (created in his image) and secondly because of what we can do.

A famous philosopher named René Descartes once said, "*Cogito ergo sum*" (I think, therefore I am). It sounds profound and it seems to have impressed a lot of people. The problem is that if God is, and we are his creatures, it's not the whole picture. To really understand who we are, we may have to discard Descartes (sorry, René, old buddy). We are who we are, even if we can't think. Who we are as human *beings* does not depend on what we do (whether it's thinking or anything else).

Okay, so what does all this have to do with the Third Commandment? Plenty. God gives us six days a week for *doing*. The

Sabbath is the one day of the week for *being.* It's a day to take to heart God's mandate to "be still and know that I am God" (Ps. 46:10). Sunday is the day to set aside our usual activities; rest from the furious pursuit of money, achievement, passions, or activities all around us; and be more spiritual, restful, and at peace.

How Do I Keep Sunday Holy?

Sure, it sounds like a great idea—slowing down and being more spiritual once a week—but how do I do this with my busy schedule? Well, one thing you can do—in fact, you are obliged to if you are a Catholic—is go to Mass. Some people don't have a choice about working on Sundays, but you could make it clear to your boss that you'd rather not work on that day. If you have a coach, a scout leader, or a band or theater director who plans activities for Sunday, you could also make it clear that you prefer not to rehearse or practice or do whatever on that day. That day could be spent with family and friends or doing nonstressful activities. Like what? Visiting a good friend; having quality time with your mom, dad, grandpa, Auntie Em; reading a good book; going surfing; watching clouds from under a tree; or taking your little brother ice-skating … the possibilities are endless. But Sunday should not be just another workday, and God makes it clear in the Third Commandment that he doesn't want it treated that way.

Back in the days of the dinosaurs, when I was a teenager, many of my Sundays were spent doing homework. Maybe it's the same for you now. But I always went to Mass; hopefully you do, too. And I was able to avoid working for money on that day. As a teen and young adult, I worked a wide range of jobs, including McDonald's, Domino's Pizza, Shakey's Pizza, a paint store, a department store, a gas station, and even a car wash. I always made it clear to my bosses that I would only work on Sunday if I absolutely had to. They always respected my wishes, and I'm glad to say I didn't work on Sunday in any of those jobs.

Keep Sunday Holy, You Frijole

As you grow older, and as you're able to take charge more and more of the shape and direction of your life, it's important that—in your own way—you keep Sunday as a restful, holy, and spiritual day of *being.* It's good psychology because you'll be able to work better when you return to your usual weekly activities. And, more importantly, it's good *spirituality* because you're obeying God's commandment. So keep the Sabbath holy, you frijole. Take a day once a week to rest, do less, and *be* with your family, your friends, yourself, and your God.

The Fourth Commandment: "Honor Thy Father and Mother"

Bottom Line: You owe thanks to those special people, and you always will, partner.

John E. B. Goode has a hot date with the varsity cheerleader everyone adores, Candi Van Talktooer. After school, he makes a reservation at Costa Armand El Egg Restaurant, makes himself look all spiffy, puts on some after-shave and heads for the door. Then, at the worst possible time, he hears his mom's voice: "John, can you please come in here and help me?" John thinks for a moment... Should he pretend he didn't hear her? Should he go and help his mom, even at risk of making him late for the big dream date of his life? What if Candi gets mad because he's late? What if his mom is hurt or something and really needs help? What would you do if you were John?

Before we finish the story, let's rewind the tape a bit. When John was a baby, even inside his mom's womb, she had to cancel a few nights out with John's dad, because she was too exhausted or nauseous to go out. Then, when John was a little baby, his mom had to end several phone conversations with good friends, or put down a book she really wanted to read, so that she could feed John or change his diaper. Then there were all the times she had to sacrifice her time and energy to take John to the doctor, or talk with his teacher about the trouble he was in. So, in comparative terms, when you consider all that John's mom had sacrificed for him, making Candi wait a little longer wasn't an outrageous thing for John to do for his mom.

Your parents might be demanding, unreasonable at times, or have other faults. But if you honestly consider all that they have done for you, you'll understand why they deserve your respect. First, they were co-creators with God in getting you here. Even if you were adopted, someone fulfilled your childhood needs, or you wouldn't be here now.

Secondly, they made sacrifices of their money, their private time, and their plans to keep you fed, safe, and away from the neighbor's pet boa constrictor (or substitute whatever dangers apply). Regardless of your parents' shortcomings, hang-ups, tendency to nag or repeat themselves, or their inability to understand you, or their lack of reasonableness or the fact that they don't ride skateboards, they're still your parents and God calls you to honor them.

What about Kids Who Grow up Out of the Box?

"That sounds very nice," some will say, "but what about kids whose parents are divorced, or abusive, or really messed up?" The answer is that you don't honor someone by going along with everything they do or pretending they don't have faults, especially if their faults are hurtful to you. You honor them by showing them respect and wishing the best for them, even if they have let you down or sinned against you because of their own issues.

Just as a mother whose son has committed a crime will visit him in prison and never give up hope he will someday do the right thing, children who honor difficult parents never give up on their respect, their thankfulness, and their hopefulness for their parents to do well in life. Because no matter how much suffering or how many problems they may cause you, you wouldn't be able to talk about your problems, or do *anything,* if you didn't exist. And if it wasn't for your parents, you wouldn't exist. And if you didn't exist, you wouldn't have a shot at everlasting happiness with God. An ancient Chinese philosopher wrote that he would like to pay his parents back for all they gave him, but he never could fill the debt—it was as great as the sky.

Past and Present

Some scripture scholars speculate God gave this commandment primarily for adult members of the community—that is, grown offspring of the Hebrew tribes. It was a common practice among nomadic desert peoples to leave very old and unproductive members behind to die when the tribe moved on. After Moses delivered the commandments, the Hebrew people learned what they probably already knew in their hearts: the practice of abandoning unproductive parents was ungodly (translate: coldhearted, cruel, bogus, and totally uncool).

So if we look at the commandment in this way, we can see its relevance by asking who the unproductive parents in our lives are. Maybe it's your dad after a bad day at work. Maybe it's your mom when she's getting on your case about your room. Maybe it's a parent who has left the family, struggled with alcoholism, or exploded in irrational anger. Even if they're not perfect, they're still your parents, and they deserve your respect and forgiveness, and even—as long as they are not telling you to do something you know is wrong—your (gasp!) obedience. You honor them by cooperating with them and accepting their guidance as lovingly as possible. Why? Because God asked you to in the Fourth Commandment, that's why!

By the way, things did work out for John and Candi. He missed his date with her that night, because he honored his mom and went to see her instead of heading out the door. Just after that, he saw that his mom had fallen and hurt herself. So, instead of a hot date with Candi, he ended up taking his mom to the hospital. But when he told Candi what happened, she was so touched by John's way of taking care of his mom, that she fell in love with him quicker than you could say: "Whatta guy!" His next date with Candi was a blast; so were all the dates after that (except for the time he accidentally spilled Coke all over her at Costa Armand El Egg). Ten years later, they were living in a nice house with five kids and a cat named Socrates. *And all this happened because John E. B. Goode followed the Fourth Commandment!*

The Fifth Commandment: "Thou Shalt Not Murder"

Bottom Line: Killing the innocent is never okay, no matter how good the reasons seem at the time.

All right, first things first: a lot of people have gotten the wrong idea about this commandment in the three thousand (or so) years since Moses brought it down from Mount Sinai. It's often translated as "thou shalt not *kill*." But there are two words for *kill* in the Greek language (the language in which the Gospels were originally written). As C. S. Lewis put it (in his speech "Why I am Not a Pacifist," published in *The Weight of Glory*) "There are two Greek words: the ordinary word *to kill* and the word *to murder*. And when Christ quotes the Fifth Commandment He uses the *murder* one in all three accounts, Matthew, Mark, and Luke." For a one-time atheist, C. S. Lewis was one smart dude when it comes to the God Rules.

The problem with the idea that this commandment forbids all killing is that it does not differentiate between murder, which it really does forbid, and killing, which is not always wrong. Let's start with some basics. What did you have for breakfast this morning? Cereal? It came from plants that had to be killed so you could feed your face. Okay, now what about lunch? A hamburger? Was it mooing at the time you chowed down? Was the father in the story of the prodigal son breaking this commandment when he said to kill the fatted calf? No way. Killing animals and plants for food is not a sin, as long as the animals are not killed in a cruel or inhumane manner.

What about killing people? Is it always wrong? Some people say it is, but that's not what this commandment means or what the Church teaches. Three kinds of killing are not forbidden by the Fifth Commandment, and when people tell you otherwise, they're mistaken and probably should read more from a clear-thinking author like C. S. Lewis.

When Killing Isn't Murder

There are three types of killing that are not considered murder—just war, self-defense, and capital punishment. Why? Because murder means intentionally killing the *innocent,* and some killing involves those who are not innocent.

- **Just War:** There have been Catholic pacifists (like Dorothy Day) and fierce warriors (like Charlemagne and St. Louis X) who lived their lives as good and faithful Catholics but differed widely on the subject of war. It's possible to call all war immoral, but this is not what the Fifth Commandment does, nor is it what the Church has taught (not now, and not in the past two thousand years). St. Thomas Aquinas, for example, taught that there can be a just war. Two wars that most reasonable people would recognize as justifiable were the Civil War and World War II. The first ended slavery in the United States, and the second stopped Hitler and Tojo from killing and enslaving millions of innocent people. Even though some people today would argue that you're committing a sin just by joining the military, that's not what the Church teaches or what Christ taught. If it were, he would have told the Roman Centurion who approached him (Matt. 8:5–13) to quit his job. Instead, he praises the man's faith in very strong terms. Contrary to what the peaceniks may try to tell you, war is not a violation of the Fifth Commandment, although some wars, and some bad conduct within wars, can be.

- **Self-Defense:** If it's possible that nations can and should defend themselves in a just war, it's also possible you can defend an innocent person—even if that innocent person is you or someone you love. If an attacker is trying to kill you or your family and your act of self-defense kills that person, you have not broken this commandment, because you didn't murder the innocent. Similarly, if a police officer kills someone who is trying to kill innocent people, he hasn't broken the Fifth Commandment.

- **Capital Punishment:** As with war, there are many good, intelligent Catholic thinkers with differing views on this subject. Some believe that capital punishment is always immoral; others, like St. Thomas Aquinas, believe it is sometimes justifiable. One thing is clear, though—the Fifth Commandment doesn't forbid capital punishment, and when people say it does, they are mistaken. If people want to argue that capital punishment is wrong, they need to use a basis other than the Fifth Commandment, because it prohibits *murder* of the *innocent*, not government execution of the *guilty*.

When Killing *Is* Murder

There are obvious murders that everyone knows are wrong, such as homicides committed by criminals. But there are some types of murder that many people, including some governments, think are okay—but they aren't. Ralph Waldo Emerson once said, "Every actual state is corrupt. Good men must not obey the laws too well" (*Essays*: "Politics"). Even if man's law says that some types of murder are okay, God's law still forbids them. Three types of murder that the government sometimes blesses are what can be called the Gruesome Threesome: abortion, euthanasia, and suicide.

- **Abortion:** This is the murder of the most innocent: kids who haven't even been born. It kills not only the unborn child, but the conscience and possibly the soul of the mother (unless she repents and returns to God) as well as the soul of the abortionist. Anyone who thinks women don't suffer from trauma after abortion needs to visit www.afterabortion.org. Despite the false claims of abortion providers like Planned Parenthood, a woman does suffer after an abortion because she has violated her own inner instinct to preserve and protect the child in her womb. She is at war with herself because she knows in her heart that she's violating God's law. If you have a friend with an unwanted pregnancy, you should encourage her to give the child to an adoption agency like Birthright International (888-220-9140, www.birthright.com). One mistake should not be followed by another that she will regret for the rest of her life.

- **Euthanasia:** Shutting down life-support machines when someone is only being kept alive artificially, sometimes called euthanasia, is not a sin. This is not taking a life so much as allowing nature to take its course. However, the kind of euthanasia that is a sin happens when doctors (who violate their own Hippocratic Oath and become Hippocratic hypocrites) actively end someone's life by withholding nourishment (as in the recent case of Terri Schindler Shiavo) or injecting lethal medicine to end someone's life. Generally, a good doctor helps an unhappy patient find reasons to live rather than collecting a fee to help the patient kill himself! This brings us to the last of the Gruesome Threesome.

- **Suicide:** There are a few cases in which giving up one's life to save others is not a sin. St. Maximilian Kolbe volunteered to die in place of another prisoner in Auschwitz. Sometimes a brave soldier has jumped on a live grenade to save the lives of his friends. Literally laying down one's life for one's friends is not the same as committing suicide out of despair, which is a grave sin. To feel despair when things go wrong is natural, but to freely and maliciously act on that emotion and end your own life is a clear violation of the Fifth Commandment. The ancient Greek philosopher Socrates reasoned that we are the property of the gods and it is wrong for property to dispose of itself. Substitute "God" for "the gods" and all of us who believe in the God of Judeo-Christian revelation can agree. God gave you life, and your life has meaning and a purpose, whether or not it is clear to you. Author Richard Bach expressed it this way, "Here is the test to find whether your mission on Earth is finished: if you're alive, it isn't." All difficulties, no matter how bad, can be overcome with time and God's grace. Committing suicide robs God of his chance to heal and make things better. It also robs those who love you (family, friends, and neighbors) of their chance to help you or be helped by you. The tremendous lessons you may have learned through your suffering, which could be used to help others, would all be lost. Instead, you would destroy your own soul and cause grief and suffering for those around you. God will take you at the moment he's ready; and it's his right to say when, not yours. If you make it yours, you're breaking the Fifth.

The Wrap

The common denominator of the Gruesome Threesome is that each one is a way of trashing God's gift of life. Abortion destroys a new child, and euthanasia and suicide deprive us of the life and grace that should come out of suffering and difficulty. All three deprive us of life given by God to help us ultimately achieve fulfillment and happiness both in this life and the next. If many people around you ignore the Fifth Commandment, then you need to be (as Pope John Paul II urged) "countercultural for Christ's sake" so that you may say, with the biblical leader Joshua, "As for me and my house, we will serve the Lord" (Josh. 24:15).

The Sixth Commandment: "Thou Shalt Not Commit Adultery"

Bottom Line: Forget what all the glossy magazines say about good sex. The only place where sex is truly good is within marriage. Who said so? God said so.

Brad and Jenny were having a candlelit dinner before going to the senior prom. They were fighting again ...

"Just remember, Brad," Jenny said, with grit in her voice, "I could name ten guys who would KILL to love me!"

"What are you having such a cow about? All I did was say hi to her." He chewed his mouthful of spaghetti and stuffed another shovelful into his mouth.

"Yeah right, just say hi! You smiled at her with that big stupid grin! And don't think I didn't hear about you talking with her in the hall after school yesterday!"

"Who told you about that?" Brad asked, pausing to wipe the spaghetti sauce.

"Give me a little credit," Jenny said. "I still have a few friends around here."

"Look, Jenny, Samantha's just a sophomore. She asked me about a math teacher I had, and I was just giving her some advice on how to pass his class! Do you really think I have that kind of interest in a geeky little sophomore?" He paused and joyfully let out a loud burp, and as he opened his mouth some sauce leaked out and started running down his chin.

"Why are you so gross? You eat like an animal! Why can't you eat like a human being?" Jenny demanded.

In one sitting, Brad's attitude toward his spaghetti dinner and toward the cute sophomore in the hall sum up modern society's attitude toward sex (not to mention eating): gorge and go where your eyes take you. The pleasure of sex, like the pleasure of eating, can deceive us into thinking it's good anywhere, any time, with anyone. But just as improper and overindulgent eating can lead to indigestion or obesity, improper or overindulgent sex (which is pretty much 99.9% of the sex that takes place among high school and junior high students) leads to unwanted pregnancy, depression, desperation, unhappiness, fear, and hostility. In short, it leads to Sin Central, and the only way out is a full-on U-turn!

In her book about teens and sexuality (*Friends: For Teens*), author Mary Rosera Joyce described how sex is like a fire and marriage like a fireplace. As long as the fire is kept in its proper place, it's good and warming for everyone. But when someone attempts to start a fire outside the fireplace, somebody always gets burned. And, under the spell of Hollywood, cable, the Internet, and sleazy magazines in almost every grocery store, modern society is full of wildfires ruining homes, causing depressions and suicides, and making many young people think there's no such thing as a good and happy marriage. There is, but we need to go back to God's way and try obeying his laws to find what it's like.

The Real Endless Love

Though a lot of powerful people try to tell you differently, God's intention for sex is simple and straightforward. It is to provide a beautiful and wonderful gift that does two things: unite one man and one woman and beget new life. That's right—sex is meant to be a holy and awesome thing, not some cheap commodity that can be bought and sold on the street with people you hardly even know. In her book, *Women and Choice,* Mary Joyce points out the two opposite extreme viewpoints about sex: the Puritan and the Playboy. One has trouble recognizing that sex is basically a good thing in the correct context; the other (far more common today) has trouble recognizing that sex needs to be restrained and controlled.

Some people say, "Hey, it's just natural feelings. Why not follow them?" But what such people often fail to recognize is that we don't just have an animal nature, like dogs in an alley. We have a spiritual nature, too, and our spiritual nature is responsible for controlling our animal nature. Nobody would arrest a dog for committing murder, because when a dog kills, it doesn't know any better. So why would people argue we should just follow our sexual urges like dogs? No way, dog. God created us as human beings with free will and the ability to reason and use our brains to control our feelings, so that's what we need to do. Or to put it another way, a twelve-year-old may feel strong urges to drive a car, but he would be stupid to act on those urges until he turns sixteen and has his license. Similarly, young people may feel sexual urges (especially with all the impure images in today's society), but God calls them to restrain those urges and channel their powerful energy in nonsexual ways until they are within the lawful bounds of marriage. If they do, they will develop the virtue of chastity, which teaches them self-control and strengthens their willpower; this can help them in many other areas of life, especially in their future marriages.

Christian marriage (not the kind defined by the government as between two women, seven dwarves, or three men in a tub ...) is a holy and beautiful thing when it's done right. Sacramental marriage provides the safest and best fireplace for natural sexuality. In it, two people give each other the most personal gift of physical love that one person can offer another. But true, Christ-centered marriage is not just a contract between a man and a woman. It's not just a business partnership or social agreement. It is a sacrament and a covenant in which two persons become one flesh, a union that lasts a lifetime. Many teens make promises of endless love only to break their promises months or years later. But only authentic and Christ-centered marriage provides real and authentic endless love. The only people who can say they have experienced endless love are those who you might think of as the dorky or boring old couples you know: parents and/or grandparents who got married and *stayed* married for years and years without messing around or starting fires where they didn't belong.

The Wider Scope

The Sixth Commandment calls us not only to avoid adultery (messing around with someone else's wife or husband) but to abstain from all acts that violate our chastity. These include sex (or even the kind of heavy petting or foreplay that may lead to it) before marriage; masturbation; seeking out and/or viewing movies, TV, magazines, or

Web sites that contain impure images; or even spending time in places where sexual temptations might be great.

It may seem as if God is asking the impossible. But he does not expect perfection (Prov. 24:16 says that even a righteous man falls seven times each day). He expects a constant and undying effort to avoid the sleaze and live a clean life. By striving to live pure lives and conquering impure thoughts, and by asking God's forgiveness when we fail—as the former party animal Mary Magdalen once did—we grow into the men and women God calls us to be. Fasting may help as well. Controlling our desires for food helps us control other desires "of the flesh." Also, Jesus once said that some demons can only be driven out by prayer and fasting (Mark 9:29).

God does not call us down a path of convenience and thoughtless entertainment, but rather on a challenging and soul-building journey through which we become his strong, wise, and courageous sons and daughters. If we ignore him and follow society's call to go in the other direction we may think we're on the path of natural fun and ease, but sooner or later we'll realize we have sold out our Lord and our souls and are starting the wrong kind of wildfire with the wrong kind of wild dog (the kind of date your mother warned you about...) So let's not go there, dog. Let's make a real, honest, and life-long effort to follow God's law, even when it's not easy, entertaining, or going with the flow.

The Seventh Commandment: "Thou Shalt Not Steal"

Bottom Line: Unless it was earned, given, or bought, you shouldn't have it.

Rob Steele III was a sophomore at Stick-'Em-Up High. He was working on his algebra homework while his dad, Rob Steele II, was working on his income tax return nearby. Rob Jr. gave up trying to learn the material and instead started texting his buddy about how they could try to cheat on the quiz the next day. Meanwhile, Rob Sr. was putting a few false statements on his return in order to get a bigger refund. As they continued with their activities, Mrs. Steele came home from the grocery store. She unloaded the bags in the kitchen, and then she noticed the extra carton of eggs the cashier hadn't seen. She smiled as she remembered how she could have told the cashier, but didn't.

In the space of one evening, all three members of the Steele family had managed to break the Seventh Commandment. Rob's dad was stealing money that wasn't his by cheating on his income tax return. Rob's mom was stealing by "forgetting" to pay for something from the store. And Rob was stealing grades from other students who had earned them honestly by cheating on a quiz. Each member of the Steele family was taking something that wasn't rightfully his or hers.

Now, if anyone asked one of the Steeles about the stealing, he or she would most likely say "everyone else does." There are two problems with this answer (actually there are more than two, but we'll just deal with two here). The person who says this is pretty much admitting the action was wrong since he doesn't try to justify what he did. He's basically saying that if everyone else does something wrong, he can, too. Even if everyone around you is doing something wrong, that does not take away your responsibility to do the right thing. At the end of your life, when all your choices are judged by God, it won't matter what everyone else was doing; what *you* did will matter. The other problem with this statement is that people who think this way tend to see only what they want to see. There are many people who live honestly, don't steal, and respect the property of others; you only have to look for them to find them. Everyone else is never *everyone* else.

What Is/Isn't Stealing?

There are some things everyone knows are stealing, but some messages in popular culture portray these actions are cool or acceptable. One example is the popular video game Grand Theft Auto. Then there are movies like *Ocean's Eleven* (and *Twelve* and *Thirteen* ...) in which the message is basically, "Stealing may be wrong, but it becomes cool if you're stealing millions of dollars." But we need to remember (and so does Hollywood) that stealing is still stealing, even if some people try to dress it up as something cool, creative, and interesting.

Then there are some things people don't think of as stealing, but are, and other things people think might be stealing, but are not. Cheering for the Pittsburgh Steelers is not stealing (but cheering for the Raiders might be ...). Betting on your favorite sports team with a friend is not stealing, but it can become stealing if you are a parent who becomes addicted to gambling and loses the means of providing for your children. In that case, you've stolen from your own children the means for them to have the comfortable and happy life they deserve. Shoplifting is definitely stealing, but if someone takes something because he is starving and needs it to survive he might not be committing a sin. What are some other forms of stealing that many people might not think of as stealing? Hold on here, because there's a laundry list coming up.

- **Cheating on a quiz or test in school** because you are taking credit away from others who earned their grades honestly.

- **Tagging or vandalizing property** because you are taking away value from people who own the property.

- **Plagiarism or copyright violations** because you are stealing another person's ideas or work without giving him credit.

- **Borrowing that becomes *de facto* ownership** because if someone lent something to you with the expectation that you would return it and you don't, you have taken it without his full consent.

The Consequences

Many people seem to steal and get away with it, which encourages other people to steal, too. But if you think about it, there are consequences to stealing. People who steal sooner or later get caught: either by the police, their teachers or professors, the FBI, the IRS, or the ASE. *The ASE?* That's right, buddy—haven't you heard of the All-Seeing Eye? Even if you can fool human eyes and human judges, you can't fool the Just Judge who sees all you do and knows everything you should own and everything you shouldn't.

The Eighth Commandment: "Thou Shalt Not Bear False Witness against Thy Neighbor"

Bottom Line: Lying is almost always wrong, but lying in order to harm another person is always a non-negotiable major sin.

Sophomore Samantha Supercool was plotting out the next party with all her buddies, the hip and popular crowd known as the Mean Girls. As Samantha was explaining how they could have their boyfriends bring in the kegs at the right time, she noticed her nemesis, Debbie Do-Right, walking by.

"Ewwww, there she goes!" She whispered to her friends. "She acts all good and smart and pristine and all, but it's just an act … You know what I heard? I heard she sleeps with the chemistry teacher to get an A." All her friends were shocked and fascinated. They looked over at Debbie walking the other way and thought they knew her secrets. Unfortunately, what they thought they knew was a lie. Samantha was just settling scores because the school's star quarterback had stopped seeing her once he started to like Debbie. Samantha knew what she was saying about Debbie was not true, but she said it anyway because she wanted to get back at her. Samantha Supercool was acting in a manner that was totally *uncool* and in violation of the Eighth Commandment.

The Lyin' King or the Honest Thing

Songwriter Billy Joel once wrote, "Honesty is such a lonely word. Everyone is so untrue." Was he being honest about how common it is for people to be dishonest? If so, it would seem that telling the truth is not common in today's world. Actually, falsehood may be the way of the world at all times, not just nowadays. The Bible describes Satan as the "ruler of this world" (John 12:31) and the "Father of lies" (John 8:44). By contrast, Christ describes himself as one who came "into the world to bear witness to the truth." And he continues, "Every one who is of the truth hears my voice" (John 18:37). Those who are under the influence of Christ are of the truth, but those who are under the influence of the "ruler of this world" can be recognized for their untrue and deceptive ways. And that's probably most of us at certain times. The question is: do we recognize where we have gone astray and try to do better? Or do lying and deception become our way of life? The Eighth Commandment is there to guide us away from that trap.

Does that mean that lying is never justified? Keep in mind that the commandment forbids lying "against thy neighbor." There may be certain rare cases in which lying to protect someone is justified: for example, during World War II, some Christians hid Jews in Nazi Germany and lied to the authorities (who were working for Hitler) about where the Jews were hiding. People working for Pope Pius XII also falsified passports in order to save the lives of Jews in Rome. In those cases, they were not bearing false witness *against* their neighbors; they were bearing false witness to save their neighbors' lives. But how often are you in situations like these? Most likely, your honest answer would be "not very often." For that reason, it's correct to say that lying is almost always wrong.

There are very few situations today in which misleading others is the right thing to do. There may be situations where you should keep information to yourself, but withholding information is not the same thing as saying false things to mislead others. Most situations today in which people think it's okay to lie are probably situations where it would be just as well to keep information to yourself.

The Tangled Web

Sir Walter Scott once wrote, "Oh, what a tangled web we weave / When first we practise to deceive." What he pointed out was that telling lies usually leads to—what? That's right. Telling more lies. Eventually deception can become a way of life because a person becomes addicted to it as an easy and quick way of solving problems; sooner or later, the liar gets caught in his own tangled web of lies. Like every sin, habitual lying involves a trade-off: sacrificing something in the future for something in the present. In this case, what you sacrifice is the trust and respect you would have gained had you acted with integrity. Sooner or later, lies catch up with you, and you will develop a reputation as a liar whose word cannot be trusted. In that sense every lie, even white lies you think are harmless and not against your neighbor, could still be a venial sin. How? Because they work against your own reputation; they could still be against your neighbor because they are against *you*.

How can you avoid the tangled web? It is important to stick to the truth. Then, if you find that you have spoken falsely, free yourself from the web by correcting the situation. Samantha Supercool could admit to her friends that she lied about the other girl and ask Debbie for forgiveness. Is this how things usually turn out? Probably not, but it's how they would turn out if Samantha decided to free herself from the web of deception spun by sinners under the influence of the "ruler of this world."

The Wider Scope

There are many ways in which people violate the Eighth Commandment, from the most trivial and small to the most obvious and serious. One of the most serious is perjury, which means lying under oath in a court of law. This is not only a sin, but a serious, punishable crime. Another clear way people violate the Eighth Commandment is slander, or lying about another person in order to harm their reputation—what Samantha did to Debbie. There is also the common practice of deception in order to get money from someone, such as when mechanics or salespeople lie about the condition of a product in order to get more money. This actually breaks two commandments, since it involves both lying and stealing.

There are other ways people speak falsely against their neighbor that we may not think of as lying. One way young people often do this is by encouraging their peers to do something wrong. When Samantha told that lie, if her friend Sarah knew it wasn't true but decided to laugh along with it and encourage the deception, then Sarah was also guilty of violating this commandment. Any time someone encourages another person to sin, they are also violating this commandment. If young people encourage each other to smoke, drink alcohol, try drugs, join a gang, have sex, vandalize or steal property, or even cheat on a test, they are violating the Eighth Commandment. Why? Because they are trying to convince another person that something evil is really good, and this is another way of bearing false witness against their neighbor. So even if you say, "That's bad" in a way that really means "that's good" and you're talking about something that really is *bad*, then you've born false witness against your neighbor.

The Wrap

So, what have we covered here? God is the source of all truth. Satan is the Father of Lies. Pick your team and play your part. You pick your team by the way you choose to live each day. The Eighth Commandment is here to tell you not to lie, especially if it harms someone else. Tell the truth, have integrity, and avoid a tangled web of deception that can snare you later. If you are a truthful man or woman, people will respect you more in this life, and God will reward you when this life is over. Yes, he will ... *Honest to goodness! That's no lie, buddy!*

The Ninth Commandment: "Thou Shalt Not Covet Thy Neighbor's Wife"

Bottom Line: Thoughts lead to actions. If it's not your spouse (and how many teens have a spouse?), you shouldn't allow your thoughts to focus too long on that other person.

David King was a manager in a steel plant in Bethlehem, Pennsylvania. He had been promoted after the former manager, Phil S. Steen, got fired. Phil had earned the nickname Goliath because of his large size and tendency to hurl insults at people he didn't like. Anyway, Goliath was fired because there were enough complaints from co-workers to get the attention of the supervisor, and one day he got caught getting stoned on the job, and that was that. David was a little young and sheepish, but he got promoted anyway after Goliath was gone.

Years later, David was the supervisor of the whole plant, and one of his managers was a guy named Uriah Heebah. Everything was fine until, one day, Dave was driving his fancy new car and he spotted Uriah's wife (Beth Heebah) sunning herself on a lounge chair. As he passed by, he allowed the sight of Beth to completely capture his attention. His mind and his sports sedan drifted from the straight and narrow. He imagined the two of them, just David and Beth Heebah, alone on a beach somewhere …

BOOM!—SKRRRRR—CRUNCH! Dave's car popped the curb and he instinctively slammed on the brakes. The car skidded into a large tree. Dave's airbag inflated and cushioned his face as he was flung forward. After a minute, he pushed the airbag out of his way and got out of the car. Behind his smashed hood, where the steam was hissing out, he noticed a large sign that had been knocked loose and was dangling from the tree he had hit. It read, "DON'T EVEN THINK OF PARKING HERE!"

Thoughts and Actions

Dave only fantasized about making it with Beth, but he still broke the Ninth Commandment, not to mention his radiator grill. God gave us this commandment to nip adultery in the bud and to guard against the natural (fallen) human tendency toward impurity. Author Richard Bach once wrote that "we magnetize into our lives whatever we hold in our thought." In other words, thoughts lead to actions. If our thoughts are good, our actions can be great. But if our thoughts are bad, our actions will be *bogus*, messed up, and most highly *uncool*.

God gave us the Ninth Commandment because he knows we tend to follow where our thoughts lead us. The guaranteed way to avoid impure acts is to learn not to *want* impure thoughts. Considering all the impure images that surround us (on TV, on billboards, on the Internet, and with the latest sleazy fashions), this may seem an impossible ideal, but nothing is impossible with God. If you really want to persevere in a quest to follow God's call to purity, you can and you will, even though you are surrounded by a culture that celebrates impurity and tries to inundate us all with it. And if you fall, as most young people sometimes do, you learn to pick yourself up, go to Confession, and try again (and, if necessary, again and again). Someone once asked a young Catholic, "Are you a practicing Catholic?" He replied, "Yes, I am. And if I keep practicing, one of these days I'll get it right!" Beyond the joke, there's a deep truth: everyone who loves the living God is sometimes capable of sinning, and he constantly strives to come back to God and become better.

Author Mary Rosera Joyce wrote in her book about teens and sexuality, "Your most important sexual organ is your brain, because it is the organ of your thoughts, values, and decisions about your sexuality." Regardless of all the false messages about sexuality that modern culture surrounds us with, Joyce is right in pointing out that true sexuality is not centered in the genitals, but in the mind and heart. A good example of this would be most priests and nuns (not the less than 1% of the clergy who were involved in the perverted acts featured in the media a few years ago). You might know some priests or nuns who are true to their vocations, effective teachers or pastors, and joyful and inspiring disciples of Christ. Their sexuality is still part of who they are, but they have chosen to express it in nongenital ways. Good priests and nuns are happy because they have learned to recognize and control their feelings and channel their energy into positive outlets. If David King had just acknowledged Beth's beauty in a clean, positive, and *brief* manner, then refocused his attention on the road, he would have had no accident, no sin, and no problem.

Attraction versus Lust and the Three-Second Rule

There is a big difference between attraction and lust. Attraction is a feeling that happens to you; lust is something you make happen. Attraction is not a sin, but it can lead to sin if you're not careful. It's natural to be attracted to beauty, whether it's a sunset, a forest, a pet, a painting, or, well, a hot-looking person of the opposite gender. If you notice beauty and praise God for his handiwork, you haven't necessarily broken the Ninth Commandment. Sin happens if you allow your natural attraction to turn into lust.

There was a young priest named Fr. Chris who spoke about what he called the Three-Second Rule. Generally, three seconds is about all you really need to appreciate someone's beauty. After that, if you're still looking or rewinding the picture in your imagination, then innocent attraction or appreciation is probably turning into lust.

Keeping the Ninth Commandment isn't an easy task for most people nowadays, but for those who make the effort, it can be done. The first step is to recognize if, when, and how you might have broken it, then ask for forgiveness and strive to do better. God is asking a lot from you, but he gives you the grace to do it unless you refuse his gift. The key is to ask for God's grace and rely on the intercession of his all-pure Mother to see you through. Be sure, be pure, and follow God's call from the top to the bottom of the Ninth (Commandment, *ya noogie*).

The Tenth Commandment: "Thou Shalt Not Covet Thy Neighbor's Goods"

Bottom Line: Those things may look great, sound terrific, or work better than yours, but they aren't yours. So admire them, then refocus.

Greedo the Gargantuan from Galapagos had gone and gambled away gobs of gains. When he had nearly lost it all, he walked along the streets of Sin City and saw a silver sports sedan sparkling in the sun. Greedo was gone in a gust of garish grand theft, Otto. Greedo's greed wasn't a gainful creed, and he ended in Cell Block G with the other bad seed. If only Greedo had been neato and followed the Tenth Commandment.

The tenth and last of the Ten Commandments is the second of the two "Don't even think about it" commandments. God knows thoughts lead to actions, and the last two commandments are there to keep us from even starting to go wrong. Just as desiring the wrong person can lead to adultery, fornication, or other less serious but still impure acts, so desiring someone else's things can lead to theft, envy, hatred, or an unhealthy and bogus desire to harm somebody whose only crime was to have nicer things than you. The Seventh Commandment says not to steal; the Tenth Commandment says not to envy someone else's things. Greedo went into foul territory the moment he started to eye the silver Beamer. He was driving off in a cloud of dust and sin quicker than you could say "Silver Streak! It's a sinnin' freak!"

Envy: The Diabolical Sin

St. Augustine once described envy as "the diabolical sin." Other sins might be the results of weakness or lack of attention; envy is different. It's the first step to becoming more like the devils. How? Think about it: how did the Devil fall from God's grace? He started by *envying*

God's greatness and wishing he could have it for himself. For that reason, envy is the first step to all kinds of other frames of mind that are basically bad, bogus, botched, bungled, and borrific (Borrific? Byeah that's bright, buddy ...) As St. Augustine pointed out, "From envy are born hatred, detraction, calumny, joy caused by the misfortune of a neighbor, and displeasure caused by his prosperity."

Let's take a closer look at that list and get a better understanding of all the things envy can lead to:

- **Hatred:** Everyone knows what this is. When you start to envy other people, unless you turn away from it, you'll end up hating them: it's the way things go.

- **Detraction:** Instead of saying good things about other people to build them up, you start trying to pull them down to your level because you feel inferior that they have what you don't. So instead of saying good things about them, you start talking smack. This is not good.

- **Calumny:** This means spreading lies about other people behind their backs. If you envy what another person has, the tendency is to try to get even with them even if it means bearing false witness against them. Then you've not only broken the Tenth Commandment, but the Eighth as well, and you may not stop until you've broken the Seventh, too. Ouch!

- **Joy caused by a neighbor's misfortune:** Christ taught us to love others as we love ourselves. This means sharing in their joys and sorrows. If your envy and hatred are so strong that you feel glad when your neighbor suffers, you're taking serious steps in the wrong direction.

- **Displeasure caused by his prosperity:** If you feel sad because your neighbor succeeds, you need a major attitude adjustment before you end up in Satan Central. If you learn to live without envy, your neighbor's joy is a cause for your joy and his sorrow is a cause for your sorrow. If you get those in reverse, you need to *put it in reverse* and back out of the bad attitude.

Each of the bad things listed above started with envy. For this reason, the antidote to envy is the Tenth Commandment: don't even think about taking your neighbor's things. Admire them, and be glad for the person who has them, but be on guard against falling into the sin of envy.

Envy and the Count

Envy doesn't just rob us of the happiness, contentment, and gratitude we should feel for the things that are ours, but it also can rob us of the joy of true friendship. A good example can be found in the classic novel *The Count of Monte Cristo* by Alexandre Dumas. In this story, a young man from a rich family (Fernand) becomes so envious of his friend from a poor family (Edmond) that he betrays his friend and lies about him; Edmond is sent away to prison and torture, even though he is innocent. Envy turns Fernand's friendship and joy into hatred and calumny. Fernand frames his friend and marries the man's fiancé, only to find he is not happy. Later, Edmond escapes from prison and becomes the count of Monte Cristo. He adopts a disguise and finds out that his former friend is cheating on his former fiancé; Fernand only wanted her when she belonged to someone else. Fernand's envy led him to a series of diabolical acts, but not to happiness. There's much more to the story, of course, but the part described here is a powerful example of the effects of envy.

Envy, like lust, is a state of mind. Even if you have not committed any acts, the state of mind is itself a sin. God sees not only all we *do*, but even all we *think*. For that reason, we need to guard our thoughts from desiring things or people that are not ours. The last two commandments have to do not with actions, or *doing*, but with attitudes of *being*. In fact, you could call them the two "be-attitude" commandments, but then you would be jumping the gun on the next part of this little book ...

Introduction to the Beatitudes

In the first section of this book, we looked at each of the Ten Commandments. Now we turn our attention to the eight Beatitudes, which were spoken by our Lord in the Sermon on the Mount. Before we begin, let's look at the Beatitudes as a group and how they are similar to—and different from—the Ten Commandments.

What they both have in common is pretty basic: they were given by God, and they show us how we should act in our day-to-day lives. They both make it clear that God should be first and foremost in all we do; basically, we should learn to live for him and should never let anything or anyone else become more important in our lives. Both the Ten Commandments and the Beatitudes were given to guide us to live as God calls us to live. They are directions for the care and usage of the products that we are, direct from the Manufacturer.

The differences have to do with the direction of their focus. As we mentioned earlier, the commandments mostly start with "Thou shalt not ..." But the Beatitudes all say you are blessed if you *do* things, not if you *don't* do them. God made clear to Moses many of the things people *shouldn't* do, but when he became one of us, he spoke more often about what we *should* do. That's not to say that Christ didn't teach us not to do things, because he most definitely did—for example, not to judge others, not to pray publicly in order to gain human approval, not to lust where our hearts don't belong, and not to seek a divorce where God has joined a man and woman in marriage. But the Sermon on the Mount, and the Gospels in general, contain a significantly greater proportion of positive commands than prohibitions when compared with the teachings of the Old Testament.

Similarly, the Old Testament often represents God as distant and to be feared. By contrast, after Christ became one of us, phrases that often appear are "do not be afraid" and "do not fear." The first was spoken by the angel Gabriel when he appeared to Mary in the Annunciation. The second was used repeatedly by our Lord when he cured those who sought healing for their illnesses. A general theme of the New Testament is that God is now inviting us to come to him out of love, rather than fear. Of course, to come to him out of fear is better than not to come to him at all, but the life and teachings of Jesus show that love for God is the highest ideal and best motivation for our approach to him. In fact, when Jesus was asked about the greatest commandment, he said, "You shall love the Lord your God with all your heart, and with all your soul, and with all your mind, and with all your strength" (Mark 12:30). Secondly, he said you should love your neighbor as yourself (Mark 12:31). The emphasis is on love for God and neighbor, rather than fear of consequences; however, that's not to say fear of consequences should have no place in our thoughts. God's self-revelation in the Old Testament is still God's self-revelation. It's a case of both/and rather than either/or. Our primary motivation should be love for God because he is all good and all loving, but there's nothing wrong with also having a sober and rational fear of the consequences of *not* loving him and our neighbor.

The world in which Christ preached the Beatitudes was a world in which mighty warrior kings were constantly conquering their neighbors and building fearsome empires; not only the Egyptians, but many others, such as the Assyrians, the Hittites, the Babylonians, the Greeks, and finally the Romans, had become great and widely feared among vast territories and different cultures and peoples, including the Jews among whom Christ was born. Generally, the only people who were widely feared and respected were rich and powerful commanders of armies and rulers of empires. In contrast, Christ, who was born in a lowly manger, preached the Beatitudes: blessed are the poor in spirit, those who mourn and are meek, the merciful and pure of heart, those who hunger for righteousness, and those who make peace and are persecuted for righteousness' sake. Clearly, he wasn't all that impressed with the powerful, the mighty, the rich, and the fearsome just because everyone else was. If we think for a moment about the world in which Christ lived and preached, we can appreciate how radically different his message about the Kingdom of God was for its time. If it seems less strange to us today, we can probably attribute that to the success of his message through the centuries: it has reached the farthest corners of the earth and transformed all of humanity to a much greater degree than most people realize. The consciousness of all of humanity is entirely different now because of Christ and the teachings of the Church for the last two millennia—since his incarnation among us. To understand why and how, the Beatitudes are worth studying.

Even if we don't live in a world where fearsome warrior kings are constantly forging empires through brutal and merciless violence, modern society still tends to pay far more attention to the "great" and the "beautiful" (rich and powerful) than it should, and far less attention to the weak and defenseless. If you take the Beatitudes to heart, your attitude will be in stark contrast to the attitude of mainstream society. For that reason, each beatitude discussed in the following pages will be introduced with a contrasting "Stream Attitude" right after it. This will give you a clear idea of the difference between Christ's beatitudes and the attitudes of the world around us.

There are two ways the first word of each Beatitude is usually translated into English: *blessed* and *happy*. This is significant because it shows that the ancient Greeks (in whose language the Gospels were originally written) believed the two terms were interchangeable. If you are blessed, you are happy, and vice versa. It goes back to the ancient Greek philosophical concept of *eudaimonea*—the concept of human happiness and wholeness discussed by Socrates, Plato, Aristotle, and many other Greek philosophers. The roots of the word are *eu,* which means good or well-being, and *daimon,* which means spirit. The ancient Greeks realized the source of true happiness was a combination of good acts (or virtue) and a spiritual focus. They understood this even without the benefit of God's direct self-revelation; the major significant moment in their spiritual history was when Paul visited them at Athens and found a statue dedicated to an "unknown god." Paul told them, "What therefore you worship as unknown, this I proclaim to you" (Acts 17:32). He then brought the knowledge of the living God to them, and the story of the Greeks has never been the same. But the pre-Christian Greek concept of *eudaimonea* shows they understood something many of us today seem to have forgotten, even though we, unlike them, have the benefit of God's full self-revelation—the concept that being truly and completely happy and being blessed by God are one and the same. Whether you say "blessed are those who ..." or "happy are those who ...," the basic idea is pretty much the same. If you do blessed things you'll be happy, and if you do the things that make you happy (really and truly happy), you'll be blessed.

So read the Beatitudes. Get to know them better. The Catechism of the Catholic Church describes them as "at the heart of Jesus' preaching" (2.I:1716). By learning them and living them, you will be blessed and happy, both in this life and beyond—as you were meant to be when you were created.

Beatitude #1: "Blessed Are the Poor in Spirit, for Theirs is the Kingdom of Heaven"

Stream-Attitude: The rich and famous are the ones who matter; if you're not, you don't.

Way back in the days when Chevy Chase was on *Saturday Night Live*, he would pretend to be a news anchorman. He once began his broadcast routine with a smug smile and looked into the camera and said, "Good evening. I'm Chevy Chase, and you … you're just a statistic!" The gag was funny, but the reality behind it was not. The prevalent attitude in today's society is that the only people who matter are the rich and powerful: the Beautiful People of Hollywood, members of the media, rap stars, sports stars, the wealthy, and the highest-ranking members of government. These people might live like kings, surrounded by luxuries, pleasures, and people who are paid to do everything they say. But their kingdom is of this earth: it dies when they die. Real and lasting happiness—both in this life and beyond—can only be found in the Kingdom of Heaven.

We all know who the rich and famous are (Why? Um, because they're, like, famous …), but what about the rest of us? We don't live like kings. We go to school or work, struggle to pay bills, take care of our families, and live lives out of the spotlight. Many young people have dreams of future glory, such as achieving fame in movies, music, sports, or some other field. But it's always best to have a Plan B, because for every person who actually makes it big, there are literally millions who have the same dreams without the success or stardom. And you don't have to make it big to be happy; you can find happiness with what you're doing right here, right now, if you make God first and foremost in your life. Instead of striving first for glory, money, fame, power, or pleasures, the key is to strive for God and to be poor in spirit.

What Does It Mean to Be Poor in Spirit?

Isn't this just a fancy way of saying poor? Not exactly. It's true that people who are materially poor are more likely to be poor in spirit, but this is not always the case. Being poor in spirit is more an attitude than a measure of what you have or don't have. There are people who have achieved great material success but have remained poor in spirit; they have used their wealth to help others and make the world a better place. A good example is Thomas Monaghan, founder of Domino's Pizza and a Catholic philanthropist who donates millions of dollars to help people in need all over the world. He has used his wealth from the pizza business to help poor people in different countries in South America, to found universities, to help prolife groups, and to fund many other worthy causes. He proves you don't have to be poor to be poor in spirit.

On the flip side of the coin, there are some people who are poor but *not* poor in spirit. Probably the clearest example are those who were influenced by the political theories of Karl Marx. He saw everything in history as a struggle between the rich and the poor, and he believed the only way to help the poor was to encourage violent revolution in order to overthrow the rich. Marx's writings reject Christianity and instead justify hatred, envy, and murder of the rich by the poor. Unfortunately, his theories became reality for millions of people in the form of communist dictatorships—and what happened whenever the poor took power in the name of Marxism/communism? The formerly poor revolutionaries quickly became the new rich and ruling class and started oppressing and killing the same people who had supported their rise to power. Author George Orwell showed this in his brilliant little book, *Animal Farm.* This happened first in Russia, then China, then in many countries in Central and South America, Africa, and Asia. All of those who rose to power through the theories of Karl Marx (including Lenin, Stalin, Mao, Castro, Saddam Hussein, and Hugo Chavez) initially acted like they would help the poor in order to get their support, but when in power they shut down freedom of expression, freedom of religion, and ended up ignoring those who were still poor. These so-called revolutionaries show that not everyone who is poor is poor in spirit.

So what does it mean to be poor in spirit? It means to be humble, which means to reject egoism, pride, self-importance, or the pursuit of any worldly ambition (wealth, power, fame, or pleasure) for its own sake. Ambition to succeed in the world is not necessarily a bad thing as long as God comes first and we remain humble and grateful to God and others for whatever success we achieve. The best example of someone poor in spirit is Christ himself. Since he is almighty God, he could have chosen any kind of birth—in a mighty palace, surrounded by wealth, or even in a billion-dollar getaway tucked in the quiet little town of Beverly Hills. But he chose a poor, humble birth—a stable, a place not built for people but for farm animals, in a town that didn't even have a zip code at the time (But there were no zip codes at that time! Shhhh ... Quiet!) He could have chosen any time and place to be born, but he didn't choose our own time—with all its modern comforts and techno-wonders—and he didn't choose a place where the mighty and powerful surrounded themselves with walls, servants, and guards. That was how the wealthy lived two thousand years ago. Today, the wealthy surround themselves with ... well ... walls, servants, and guards (the guards nowadays are the ones with dark sunglasses and permanent frowns). By contrast, St. Paul described Christ, "who, though he was in the form of God, did not count equality with God a thing to be grasped, but emptied himself, taking the form of a servant, being born in the likeness of men. And being found in human form he humbled himself and became obedient unto death, even death on a cross. Therefore God has highly exalted him and bestowed on him the name which is above every other name" (Phil. 2:6). What was true then is still true today: "Whoever exalts himself will be humbled, and whoever humbles himself will be exalted" (Matt. 23:12).

True versus False Humility

Some people think being humble means denying your own worth or pretending you don't have gifts. But this is really false humility, and it can become another form of pride—self-righteousness. Being truly poor in spirit means being down-to-earth and truthful, not putting on an act by denying things about you that are true, even if they are good. You don't have to go around screaming, "We're not worthy!" as if you were Bill and Ted (or was that Wayne and Garth?) in order to be humble.

Harmful/Harmless Pride

Some people think there's nothing wrong with pride. But there are many different kinds of pride. A lot of things people describe as pride aren't necessarily sins; for example, pride in one's country, pride in one's children, or refusal to be ashamed of one's religious faith. None of these are what Christian writers mean when they warn us about the sin of pride. If you notice, each of them refers to pride in something or someone *outside* of oneself. The kind of pride that can kill (a soul) focuses on oneself, and instead of causing a person to be grateful to God for all that one has and is, it inverts gratitude into attitude. C. S. Lewis wrote (in his book *Mere Christianity)*, "According to Christian teachers, the essential vice, the utmost evil, is Pride. Unchastity, anger, greed, drunkenness, and all that, are mere fleabites in comparison: it was through Pride that the devil became the devil: Pride leads to every other vice: it is the complete anti-God state of mind." In the famous poem *Paradise Lost*, the Renaissance poet John Milton describes Satan uttering the words, "Better to reign in hell than to serve in heaven." Satan became proud when he stopped serving God and started serving himself. The antidote to the deadliest sin is humility: being poor in spirit. Christ, who was the greatest model of someone poor in spirit, showed us the way when he prayed, "Thy will be done." (This was not only something he taught in the Our Father (Matt. 6:10); it was also the prayer he made in the Garden of Gethsemane the night before he was crucified (Luke 22: 42). You are poor in spirit if you put God's will before your own will; if you don't, you aren't.

The Wrap

Even though the world says the poor in spirit don't matter because they don't go after worldly kingdoms, Christ says they are blessed because they have the Kingdom of Heaven, which is both a reward after death and a state of mind that fosters happiness and peace even in this world.

How else can we define what it means to be poor in spirit? Some helpful quotes follow:

- "He leads the humble in what is right, and teaches the humble his way." (Ps. 25:9)

- "Pride goes before destruction, and a haughty spirit before a fall." (Prov. 16:18)

- "What does the Lord require of you, but to do justice, and to love kindness, and to walk humbly with your God?" (Mic. 6:8)

- "It was pride that changed angels into devils; it is humility that makes men as angels." (St. Augustine)

Finally, here's one from the Epistle of Peter; it's sort of an antidote to the messages from popular culture about how disrespect for older people is cool or acceptable:

- "Likewise you that are younger, be subject to the elders. Clothe yourselves, all of you, with humility towards one another, for 'God opposes the proud, but gives grace to the humble.' Humble yourselves therefore under the mighty hand of God, that in due time he may exalt you." (1 Pet. 5: 5-6)

Beatitude #2: "Blessed Are Those Who Mourn, for They Shall Be Comforted"

Stream-Attitude: Big girls don't cry, real men don't show feelings; if that's water in your eye, it better be those onion peelings.

"Peelings ... Nothing more than peelings ..." Oh, that's not how the popular song goes? Whoops. Let's try opening this discussion in a different way ...

Modern society often tells us crying is a sign of weakness. When people cry, we often hear phrases like "you wimp" or "don't be a baby." American culture is rooted in Puritanism, an unbalanced religious mode never comfortable with feelings. Despite all the progress we've made in understanding ourselves, tears and sorrow are still often seen as a sign of weak character. But nothing could be further from the truth.

Let's focus on a certain dark moment in recent history. Why? Because no one who lived through it could be called a wimp, a sissy, or a person of weak character. Between 1941 and 1945, millions of Jews and Christians were systematically put to death in concentration camps under orders of Hitler's Nazi regime. If there was a place where only the strong survived, this was it; and sometimes not even the strong did. Two young men, one a Jew and one a Catholic, survived the Nazi death camps and went on to become well-known psychiatrists and authors (Victor Frankl and Conrad Baars). Both wrote books documenting their incredible suffering and soul searching. They both declared their tremendous suffering taught them something mainstream psychiatry and psychology did not—that man is a spiritual being, not an irrational animal or a soulless, genetically predetermined machine. For unless we are spiritual, there is no substantial reason why a life of immense suffering is still worth living.

The most well-known book by Victor Frankl (the Jewish psychiatrist), *Man's Search for Meaning,* focuses on the need for people to find a meaning for their lives in order to have a reason to keep living. He also pointed out how, contrary to conventional wisdom, tears indicate strength, not weakness, because they show a person's soul has strong attachments to other souls and to the suffering soul of God. These same feelings that move us to cry also help us to endure hardship, remain hopeful, and love others more deeply and completely than we could otherwise.

Conrad Baars (the Catholic psychiatrist) insisted it was only his faith in God and his inner emotions of fear, anger, and sorrow that kept him alive until he was liberated from the death camp in 1945. It is through our sorrows and tears that we really grow in wisdom and grace. Yes, we grow through our joys and triumphs, too, but not as much as through our sufferings. C. S. Lewis put it beautifully in his book *The Problem of Pain* when he declared that God whispers to us in our joys but shouts to us in our sufferings.

So who are those who mourn? We know young children cry when they don't get their way. Shakespeare's King Lear declares, "When we are born, we cry that we are come to this great stage of fools." All of us are children of God, and just like little kids, we mourn when things don't go our way: when a loved one dies, when we feel betrayed, when we are caught doing something embarrassing, or when we fail in something that means a great deal to us. We are conditioned by advertising and the media to think we can only be happy if everything goes our way. "The trend of the day," Mother Teresa once said, "is toward materialism, overindulgence, luxury, amusement." No wonder so few people seem to understand the strength and importance of mourning!

No matter how much you have, real life always has its unavoidable disappointments. No new and improved product will ever change that. And just as a child grows up to realize he can't always have his own way, so we all eventually realize—unless we're in denial—the whole universe does not revolve around us. God's will is often not our will. We are blessed when we mourn because we have a great opportunity to grow in God's grace by accepting God's will. When we suffer and cry, our souls become cleansed and at peace. The ancient philosopher Aristotle described the purpose of tragedy, as an art form, as achieving a sort of cleansing of the soul through the expression of tears and sadness. After the inner storm of tears subsides, there's calm and an opportunity for God to enter in. This is when we are ready to be comforted—by others and, through prayer, by God.

What did Christ mean by saying those who mourn would be comforted? Just as thirst is followed by drinking, mourning is followed by comfort. God moves to comfort us sometimes through the love of others, and sometimes directly through his grace. After Jesus suffered and cried in the Garden of Gethsemane, he accepted his Father's will (his own suffering and death), and an angel was sent to comfort him. When we mourn, we set the stage for someone to comfort us. If we never face our grief in mourning, our hearts become hardened, and we can become heartless, soulless, robotic machines. The Bible warns us not to let our hearts become like stones. Unless we allow ourselves to mourn, how else can we be comforted?

Tears and sorrow are a necessary and blessed part of our growth toward God. As George Macdonald pointed out: "The Son of God suffered unto death, not that men might not suffer, but that their sufferings might be like His" (*Unspoken Sermons, First Series*) And when Christ makes our sufferings like his own, he makes our souls more like his own and draws us closer to heaven—our ultimate purpose in life, our ultimate joy and the end to all our sorrows, where "he will wipe away every tear from their eyes, and death shall be no more, neither shall there be mourning nor crying nor pain any more, for the former things have passed away" (Rev. 21: 4).

Beatitude #3:
"Blessed Are the Meek, for They Shall Inherit the Earth"

Stream-Attitude: I'm the best, the baddest, the meanest there is. I'm a catalogue of crime and I'm takin' what's mine!

Bulk Bogus the Bad was boasting 'bout bashing the bones of Boston Bart Braggadoccio on WBBS (Wotta Brutus Broadcast Sleaze), a cable network. "And then I'm going to tear his face off, and keep it as a trophy, because I'm the biggest and the baddest there is, and he's nothin'!" As he spewed the words of self-promotion and senseless hate, he snarled and pointed his grimy finger at the camera. He leaned so close that his finger made sweaty marks on the camera lens. The camera operator winced and offered him a breath mint.

Meekness? No. Flagrant egoism, exhibitionism, unthinking hatred acted out for applause and money. Unfortunately, that's what a lot of people pay to see. But it sure wasn't what Christ was talking about when he said, "Blessed are the meek."

Bogus versus Cristus

While Bulk Bogus personifies a current popular icon of egoism, the best example of meekness is the Christ of the Gospels. Throughout history, all kinds of great leaders have glorified themselves and ignored Christ: King Henry VIII, Napoleon Bonaparte, Adolph Hitler, Joseph Stalin, and Chairman Mao are all clear and well-known examples. (Actually, most of them didn't just ignore Christ; they hated his teachings and killed his followers by the millions.)

In contrast to these murderous and destructive tyrants, think about the example of Jesus Christ. There are numerous examples of his humility; in fact, he was even born in a stable! He didn't insist on his own way, but always submitted to his Father's will;

one of his signature statements was "thy will be done." He always showed caring and compassion toward others, even his enemies. When people attacked and questioned him, he was sometimes silent and at other times challenged them with stern words, but he never hated, slandered, or lied about anyone. When he was angry, it was not out of concern for what others were doing to *him* but out of a deep love for those who were (literally) on a highway to hell. He was acting out of concern for what they were doing to *themselves*. But he never let his justified hatred for actions become hatred for persons. He hated the sins, but loved the sinners. Think about it: Jesus never ran for office, never used his powers or his widespread reputation to his own advantage. He never wrote a screenplay or even thought of forming a band called Woodworker and the Fish-dogs. Instead, he stayed true to the will of his Father and submitted himself to his Father's plan at all times. He lived, loved, taught, suffered, and died for sinners like you and me. As St. Paul wrote, 'Though He was in the form of God, Jesus did not deem equality with God something to be grasped at. Rather, He emptied Himself and took the form of a slave, being born in the likeness of men. He was known to be of human estate and it was thus that He humbled Himself, obediently accepting even death, death on a cross!" (Phil. 2:6)

Seek to Be Meek

Meek isn't a common word nowadays. Maybe it sounds too much like *geek* or *freak*, which turns people away ... No, that's probably not it. The current neglect of the word *meek* probably has more to do with what the word means—being humble, mild, and gentle. And these days, it seems like hardly anyone wants to be this way. We replace our simple trust and faith in God with our own power-hungry wills. In his short but wisdom-packed book *The Great Divorce*, C. S. Lewis says that in the end, there are basically two kinds of souls: those who say to God "thy will be done" and those to whom God finally says "thy will be done." Which kind do you think are the meek? The most famous description of Satan in all literature (other than the Bible) is in the poem *Paradise Lost* by John Milton. In it, the Latin phrase *non serviam* was spoken by Satan to God. It literally means, "I will not serve." Satan then declared he would rather reign in hell than serve in heaven. What kind of person makes that choice?

Anyone who sells his soul for power, money, or glory rather than offers it in obedience and service to God. Is this something you could end up choosing? Well, you're reading about his laws right now, which is a good sign you're not gong to end up like Satan, Hitler, Stalin, or Bulk Bogus the Bad ... But only you can decide the ultimate answer to that question.

Jesus knew the real road to happiness and fulfillment lies not in our own egos and power but in meekness, humility, and obedience to God's will. Jesus gave us this Beatitude (and all his teachings) for *our* benefit. This doesn't mean there aren't proper kinds of ambition and that we can't accomplish great things in this world; it means that whatever we do, we do for God's glory and not our own. And we recognize it's his power, not our own, that accomplishes all the good we do. In Shakespeare's play *Henry V*, the great king—whose army has just won the Battle of Agincourt against an opposing army five times its size—gives the command, "Let there be sung *Non nobis* and *Te Deum*." The Latin text of the *Non nobis* hymn is, "*Non nobis, Domine, Domine, non nobis, Domine / Sed nomini, tuo da gloriam*. This translates as, "Not to us, O Lord, not to us / But to your name give glory." King Henry wanted to give the glory and credit to God, not himself, and that's what made him a great king (at least in Shakespeare's play). He commanded an army but retained meekness before God. Other famous examples of people who retained meekness, despite certain amounts of fame and fortune, are George Washington, Mahatma Gandhi, and Mother Teresa of Calcutta.

Inherit the What?

The meek shall inherit the earth. You mean if I'm gentle and obedient to God's will and stuff, like, I'm gonna get some real estate? Okay, cut the camera, stop the tape, take five ... Obviously, Jesus didn't mean everyone who's meek will get a plot of land.

Some scholars interpret "inherit the earth" to mean inherit the land, as in the Promised Land, which could symbolize the kind of peace and happiness that come from the Kingdom of God. By being meek and submissive to God's will, we inherit God's Kingdom, which includes the earth and everything else. The Kingdom of God exists here and now as a state of mind for those who are meek before God.

So be meek, geek, and inherit the earth, the land, the Promised Land!

Beatitude #4:
"Blessed Are Those Who Hunger and Thirst after Righteousness, for They Shall Be Satisfied"

Stream-Attitude: God's righteousness doesn't exist or doesn't matter. All that matters are the Four Pernicious *P*s: pleasure, power, phame, and phortune."

Jim Morrison, John Belushi, and Freddy Mercury ... what did these celebrities all have in common? A) Talent, drive, a sky-rocketing career, and millions of dollars. B) A tragic early death. C) Both of the above. If you answered *C*, you are correct.

What else did each of these famous people have in common? They all hungered and thirsted for different things, but not the righteousness of God. Morrison was the lead singer of the popular '60s rock band The Doors and was the ultimate rock idol of his generation. He furiously pursued a life of sexual and drug-induced pleasures until his tragic overdose in 1971. John Belushi's great talent for comedy will live on in the original *Saturday Night Live* episodes and the quirky 1980 film *The Blues Brothers*. But his personal life was about as indulgent and immoral as Morrison's, and he died of an overdose in 1981. Ten years later, rocker Freddy Mercury of the British group Queen, the man whose voice still echoes around the world whenever a victorious sports team plays "We are the Champions," met his death in 1991, a victim of AIDS. Another life of Bohemian Rhapsody was stamped out by its own wandering feet.

Morrison, Belushi, and Mercury (and more recent celebrities who suffered similar deaths, like Curt Cobain and Michael Jackson) all hungered and thirsted for pleasures, fame, and worldly success. Everyone talks about their deaths as tragedies, and they were; but the real tragedies are their chosen lifestyles of unquenchable desires and unstoppable self-destruction. Morrison once sang, "We chased our pleasures here / Dug our treasures there ...," but when he continued, "Break on through to the other side..." it's not likely the "other side" he was talking about referred to heaven. Did these tragic stars find mercy and forgiveness after death? God only knows. But we do know they never reached their potential while on Earth, and their aimless searching only caused self-destruction. While we may enjoy the entertainment they produced, we have to feel sorry for them.

Hunger for the wrong things will never be satisfied. The route to happiness and fulfillment cannot be found in the four Pernicious *P*s: pleasure, power, phame, and phortune. These things are not necessarily evil in and of themselves, but they become evil if they are pursued instead of the righteousness of God. And that's a dance that too often ends in death. It's no wonder Pope John Paul II once referred to modern culture as a Culture of Death and challenged young Catholics to build a Culture of Life.

Total Righteousness: The Real Quencher

"So if we avoid hungering and thirsting for the Pernicious Ps," you might say, "how do we hunger and thirst after righteousness? And what is this most awesome righteousness thing, dude?" *Righteousness* is basically the old word meaning "what is right." For a Christian, it means to love and serve God above everything else and to love others as you love yourself. A thirst for righteousness is also a thirst for justice, even among people who are not Christians.

This raises the question: can non-Christians be righteous? They can, but it may not come to them as clearly. All people have an inner voice or conscience that pulls them toward righteousness, and it pulls them toward God even though they may not recognize the source of the goodness in their hearts. Many people ignore this inner voice, but others have followed it with a passion, even outside the fellowship of Catholic-Christian faith. People who have hungered and thirsted for righteousness without professing Christianity include Abraham Lincoln, Mahatma Gandhi, Anwar Sadat, and Aung San Suu Kyi. Non-Catholic Christians in this category include Dietrich Bonhoeffer,

Dr. Martin Luther King, Jr., and Aleksandr Solzhenitsyn. If you study the lives of any of these people, you will find a hunger and thirst for righteousness in their words and actions. Many of them gave their lives for the righteousness to which they devoted themselves.

As there are people who serve God without fully knowing it, there are people who are saved through Christ even if they do not learn to profess his name until their death. That is what is meant by the Church's teaching about Baptism of Desire. Of course, it's better to fully know and understand who God is, which is why missionary activity is still important. But good people of all faiths or none are capable of thirsting for righteousness.

The Heavenly Payoff

But what about people who hunger and thirst for righteousness and never seem to have their fill? What about people who have to live with bad things all through their lives? What about people who live and die in slavery or oppression? When do they have their fill?

There are two ways that God can fulfill his promises. One is on this planet, in this life. The other is in a world connected to this one by faith, grace, angels, saints, and a number of long-distance prayers—heaven. The Kingdom of God exists in both worlds, as do its rewards. Some people only receive their fill of righteousness after death; others begin to receive it in this life, although it's not yet perfect or complete. For the millions of people who don't receive their fill of justice in this life—the innocent children who die from abortion, the kids who get killed for refusing to join gangs, people in other countries who die in prisons for speaking against oppressive governments—God still has an answer. It is heaven: a place where all their suffering is only a memory and their fill of righteousness and happiness becomes perfect and lasts forever. In the heavenly kingdom, all injustice, emptiness, loneliness, pain, and doubt bite the dust and give way to the fulfillment of perfect love with God.

In the Fourth Beatitude, Jesus assures us that our reward in heaven will be great if we hunger and thirst for righteousness instead of the Pernicious Ps. We can make it if we choose to begin living it here and now. We won't get there by following the self-destruction of Morrison, Belushi, or Mercury, who hungered and thirsted for the wrong things. We will get there by thirsting for righteousness, as did the thousands of saints and martyrs before us. So thirst your worst for God's way first. Pay God's bill, do his will, and get your fill (even if your name's not Phil, or Bill, or Jill ...)

Beatitude #5:
"Blessed Are the Merciful, for They Shall Attain Mercy"

Stream-Attitude: It's a dog-eat-dog world out there, dog. People have been mean to me, so why shouldn't I be mean to them?

"Hey, Nerdly!" yelled Cooljock. "Did your mommy make you wear those glasses, or what?" All of Cooljock's buddies started laughing as Thomas Hurdley walked by. Thomas didn't notice, but Cooljock's number one lieutenant was walking right behind him. Suddenly, Thomas felt a hand slam into his back as Fooljock slapped on a post-it that said "Kick me."

"Wassup, Nerdley?" Fooljock laughed. "I'm glad to see your back!" All the guys roared with laughter, as Thomas kept walking, trying to ignore them. Cooljerk and Fooljerk started kicking Thomas while the other cool fools joined in with taunting and laughter. Thomas dropped one of his books and bent down to pick it up; as he did, one of the guys pushed him into the bushes, where he landed on the ground, and the rest of his books spilled all over the grass.

Then something weird happened. As all the other cool fools were laughing and taunting Thomas, Cooljock suddenly stopped laughing and looked at Thomas trying to get up and gather his scattered books. Cooljock actually started to feel sorry for Thomas. For a moment, he thought about his image and how his friends expected him to act a certain way with nerds like Thomas. Then he remembered something he had heard about "Blessed are the geeks," or something like that. He said to himself, "Wait a minute, who's the leader here—these other cool fools or me?" The next moment he shocked his buddies by saying, "Okay, that's enough!" The laughter quieted down on cue. The other guys looked a bit confused. Then Cooljock really shocked them by walking over to Thomas, helping him pick up his books, and taking the "Kick me" sign off his back. As the other guys scratched their heads and exchanged dumb glances with each other, Cooljock told Thomas, "Sorry, dude, we were just goofing around. Didn't mean to hurt you. See you later, guy."

Thomas was too stunned to say anything. He tried to smile at Cooljock and then turned and walked off. Cooljock went back to his friends. He realized they felt betrayed, so he thought up an excuse for what he had done. "That dude told me yesterday he was going to help me pass Dr. Meano's biology class." The homies were confused, but somewhere, high over their heads, behind a cloud, the angels were celebrating. A soul that had lost its way was turning around. What happened next? Maybe Cooljock decided it was more important to use his strength and popularity to help people instead of put them down. The rest of his life was an open book, just like yours. One thing was clear, though. He had taken a step in the right direction by showing mercy, and while it may have confused his friends, it was a cause for him to be blessed by God and possibly the first step toward a lifetime of happiness and fulfillment.

Who Are the Merciful?

The merciful could be any people who decide to show mercy to others. The merciful can even refer to people who may not be used to showing mercy, people who have spent much of their lives trying to be cool, tough, scary, or strong in the eyes of the world. *Anyone* can decide to change his past behavior and become a better person, just as Cooljock did. No matter who you are or what you do, there will be people in your life who would benefit from your decision to be merciful. They might be the nerds, the geeks, the outcasts at your school or work; they might be a brother or sister who is feeling bad about losing a friend or doing badly in their classes. They might be poor or diseased people you have never met but can help by donating to a charitable organization that feeds them or serves their needs. If you are not used to showing mercy to others, it may seem difficult or strange at first, but like many good habits, the more you do it, the easier it becomes.

A little over 400 years ago, William Shakespeare wrote a play that has one of the most beautiful and beloved descriptions of mercy of all time. See if you can figure this out:

The quality of mercy is not strained.

It droppeth as the gentle rain from heaven

Upon the place beneath. It is twice blest:

It blesseth him that gives and him that takes.

'Tis mightiest in the mightiest; it becomes

The throned monarch better than his crown.

His scepter shows the force of temporal power,

The attribute to awe and majesty,

Wherein doth sit the dread and fear of kings.

But mercy is above this sceptered sway;

It is enthroned in the hearts of kings;

It is an attribute of God himself;

And earthly power doth then show like God's

When mercy seasons justice.

(Act IV, Scene 1, *The Merchant of Venice*)

Confused? Okay, let's unpack it for you (the merciful thing to do, right?). The character in the play (Portia—pronounced like the car, but spelled differently) who gives this speech makes these points about mercy: 1) it's not forced or stressful; 2) it blesses both people who show it and people who receive it; 3) it's a powerful quality in powerful people; 4) it's a quality of the most powerful being there is, God; and 5) people become like God when they show mercy instead of demanding absolute justice. A few lines later, Portia says that "in the course of justice, none of us should see salvation." This means that none of us is perfect, and we all sometimes fail to live up to our own standards. So we all stand in need of God's mercy and sometimes the mercy of our fellow man.

Mercy versus Mushy

Ever since Shakespeare's time—in fact, going back to the time of Christ—the world has been more and more impressed with the Christian message about mercy. Unfortunately, the world doesn't always get it right. Popular culture in America for the last several decades has been shaped by a warped idea of mercy that might better be described as mushy. It comes from the secular humanist outlook that dominates much of the media, government, and academia and tries to deny the reality of good and evil. After all, if there's no real right and wrong, then people who do bad things are not doing wrong; they're just "having a behavior disorder" or "trying to compensate for being abused." Dozens of books by so-called experts in raising children (some who have never actually raised their own children) try to tell parents they shouldn't punish or spank their children when they do bad things. But this is not real mercy; it's the mushy idea that showing mercy means refusing to discipline those who need it.

This false idea of mercy isn't just found in pop-culture books and articles about raising children. It affects policies in schools and courts across the country. Teachers are sometimes told not to punish students who act disrespectful or do bad things in class. Laws are sometimes put into place that excuse criminals or put dangerous people back onto the streets. Some people think this is what Christianity is all about, but they're wrong. Christ didn't say "blessed are the mushy." The Bible also says, "He who winks the eye causes trouble, but he who boldly reproves makes peace" (Prov. 10:10). Being merciful doesn't mean being stupid or allowing evil to triumph. Even a popular song in the 1980s ("Only a Lad," written by Oingo Boingo's Danny Elfman, the same guy who wrote the theme songs of *The Simpsons* and dozens of other shows and films) understood this. The lyrics describe a young man who keeps getting away with hurting other people and doing bad things because those in authority refuse to punish him. After he steals and injures a lady, he gets away with it, then goes on to steal a car: "And when he stole the car / Nobody dreamed that he would try to take it so far/ He didn't mean to hit the poor man / Who had to go and die / It made the judge cry." Later, the lyrics satirize the mushy idea of mercy: "It's not his fault that he can't behave / Society's made him go astray / Perhaps if we're nice he'll go away." Being merciful doesn't mean being foolish or refusing to discipline or punish those who need it. Besides, showing mercy is an *individual* act; it's not meant to be a government policy.

To be merciful is to give people who are truly sorry for their sins a chance to do better—to hate the sin, but love the sinner. The problem with modern society's idea of mercy is that it doesn't hate the sin and doesn't even really love the sinner. There is a time and place for punishing and applying justice to those who have done serious evil, but there is a time and place for showing mercy, too. The devils who constantly try to trap our souls would like us to fall into one extreme or the other: to become either merciless or mushy. The way of Christ is in the middle between these two extremes. He was merciful to those who repented, but He was tough on those who didn't admit their faults and therefore refused to repent. Another excellent example of this is found in the famous French novel *Les Miserables*, by Victor Hugo. (Okay, if you're not going to read the novel, at least rent the DVD with Liam Neeson in the starring role.) In this story, Police Inspector Javert constantly pursues the escaped convict Jean Valjean, who was imprisoned for twenty years because he stole a loaf of bread when he was hungry. The inspector has a twisted idea of justice without mercy in which the law must always be followed absolutely, without any regard for human imperfection. Javert is like a cop who would cite someone for going five miles an hour over the speed limit. After years of eluding capture, Jean Valjean has a chance to kill Javert but decides to let him go. Javert can't understand why, and when he finally does catch and arrest Valjean, he decides to show mercy to him even though it violates his whole life's training. To say more than this would ruin the story if you haven't read or seen it, but it's great example of the power of mercy and forgiveness in a world that often shows no mercy and doesn't understand forgiveness.

The Wrap

"Blessed are the merciful" means that people are blessed by God when they show mercy to others. We will always need more mercy from God than others will need from us, and the way to God's mercy is by showing mercy to others. This goes hand in hand with the line in the Our Father that asks God to forgive our trespasses as we forgive those who trespass against us. It also relates to the parable of the unmerciful servant (Matt. 18: 21–35), in which the king generously forgives the debts of one of his servants, who in turn refuses to forgive the much smaller debt owed him by another servant. When the king hears about it, he gets furious with the servant whose debt he forgave and has him cast into prison. We don't want that from the King who rules us all, so we had better show mercy to the others he places around us. By being merciful we obtain mercy. Makes sense, eh?

Beatitude #6:
"Blessed Are the Pure in Heart, for They Shall See God"

Stream-Attitude: God's nice on Sunday, as long as it's not Superbowl Sunday, but most of the time I'd rather focus on booze, babes, and bucks, buddy!

Schneeborg the Zonkalator, an alien, was out cruising through space in his SUV (space-cruising utility vaporizer). He passed Planet Claire and Planet X on his way to check out Planet Earth. He was on vacation from his home planet, Yuppie-Zeitgeist-O-Rama, and he was feeling just fine. Then something went wrong and suddenly he was upset …

"Hey!" screamed Schneeborg's Right Head to his Left Head. One of Right Head's arms flailed through the air and accidentally poked Left Head in its third left eye.

"Ouch! What's the big idea?" Left Head recoiled, then promptly reached over with one of its arms to shove Right Head, who responded by using four of its arms in an attempt to throttle Left Head. As he was being choked by Right Head, Left Head started pounding and poking Right Head with all six of his arms. Schneeborg's talking heads were getting into another fight. Meanwhile, the ship started drifting into Earth's atmosphere, and as the two heads were working each other over, the ship's intergalactic radio monitor started picking up broadcasts from Earth. The heads paused from their fight and started listening to the radio.

After some static, words could be heard: "*ZZZZZZ-WEEEER-WUUUOOOOW!* You gotta have it! Why pay more? *ZZZZ-FZZZZ* … Double your pleasure. Double your money back. Double trouble. Calvin Doir Jeans. Don't ask why, just buy, buy, buy! Car insurance … Life insurance … Insurance insurance. Refinance your mortgage. Refine your face. Refine your attitude, buddy! Lose weight. Don't wait. Try the best. Get the latest. Operators are standing by. Call now! Act now! But hurry! For a limited slime only!"

The heads smiled and shook each others' hands. "This is our kind of place!"

Schneeborg's ship touched down near a huge shopping mall. He became an instant celebrity, bought a large quantity of products, and started signing contracts to endorse everything. He hired an agent, a manager, a manager's agent, and another manager to manage the manager's agent. He had two heads, but he would soon need a few hundred. That's how many directions his attention was now focused.

Making Pure

Schneeborg was going places, but heaven wasn't one of them. He had no time for the things of God. And it really didn't matter anyway, because Schneeborg wasn't made for heaven. He was made to illustrate the opposite of what it means to be pure of heart. Sometimes we who were made for heaven become like Schneeborg, which is why we need to remember Christ's words and make the ongoing, lifelong effort to be pure of heart. This means setting our hearts on God first. Whenever life sweeps us up into a stream of thoughts, images, desires, and emotions, we need to pull back and turn off all the noises and images around us and take time to be still and place God at the center of all we do. It doesn't mean everything will slow down for us, or that we won't have to work hard and perform under pressure (either in school or in a job, or both). However, it does mean that we offer all we do to God, and we should never forget how to pull back from the World (and that could mean … gasp! … less or no TV, Internet, radio, iPod, texting, or whatever) and keep our hearts pure and focused on the source of all that is good, true, and beautiful—the living God.

St. Augustine was a famous convert who had lived like Schneeborg (following all the pleasures and passions of life without God) until he converted to the Catholic faith back in the fourth century, AD. After his conversion, he wrote his famous *Confessions,* which relate the sinful life of his youth before he discovered the Christian faith. One of his most famous statements was, "Our hearts are restless until they rest in You, O Lord." What Augustine wrote some seventeen centuries ago still holds true today: no amount of TV watching, drugs, drinking, sex, money, or possessions will grant us true and lasting peace because that kind of peace comes from God alone, and not all the other stuff. Until we set our hearts on God, we will have restless and unsatisfied hearts. In another part of Matthew's Gospel, Christ encourages us to get our priorities straight: "But seek first his kingdom and his righteousness," and God will provide all the things we need (food, clothing, shelter, etc.).

To be pure in heart means to be connected to the most pure thing there is—the Kingdom of God. Its purest and most complete form is heaven, but it also exists incompletely in the midst of this world. Where? In the minds and hearts of those who belong to Christ and find the peace the world cannot give. We can begin and grow in the process of belonging more and more to God by purifying our hearts here and now. Sin and impurity obscure our vision of God, but the more pure we are, the more we see God, even if our seeing is imperfect and incomplete. And the more we purify ourselves by turning from all that is impure, as well as through prayer, reading scripture and other worthwhile things, and participating in the Sacraments of Reconciliation and Communion, the more likely we will see God completely and perfectly in heaven.

Schneeborg versus PHB

To compare Schneeborg's attitude with the attitude of someone who is pure in heart, let's introduce a character named PHB (which stands for Pure Heart Buddy). Some people think these initials stand for "PH Balanced" and have to do with hair or something, but here it means a pure-hearted approach to life. The following is a description of Schneeborg's attitude as it compares with the balanced, focused, and properly ordered attitude of someone who takes to heart Jesus's teachings: someone we'll call PHB…

Schneeborg: "My will be done. That's all that matters to me! Every feeling I experience I must act out, pursue, and gratify, NOW! I gotta see it all, do it all, and experience it all—good or bad, right or wrong."

PHB: *"Thy will be done. I care for others as I care for myself in God's name. I do without some things and refuse to do some acts if they are wrong. I control feelings that would lead me to impure thoughts and acts."*

Schneeb: "Purity, schmurity. I lust after every Zonkalatorette I see. I have dents in my SUV and dents in my soul from all the times I've wandered off the straight and narrow, and I don't care ..."

PHB: *"I guard my thoughts and perceptions. I avoid places, sights, and sounds that advertise or applaud impurity. I find more worthwhile ways to focus my attention than TV, steamy movies, or sleazy magazines. I carefully select what I will see, read, or listen to."*

Schneeb: "*Moola*, babe. That's all that's important in life. I wanna have the right car, the right looks, a summer home or two, and a hot tub in my limo. I don't have time to think about the homeless, the needy, the orphans, or the widows."

PHB: *"I see each needy, hungry, or lonely person as Christ in disguise. I weigh the needs of others as equal to mine. I'm willing to do without some of the things I want so others can have the things they need."*

Unlike Schneeborg, you only have one head, one heart, and one soul. This means you will eventually focus your life on one of two possibilities: God's will, or your own. Once again, the quote from C.S. Lewis's *The Great Divorce* applies here: "There are only two kinds of souls: those who say to God, 'Thy will be done,' and those to whom God says, 'Thy will be done.' " So which group is happier? The first one? Right you are. Be sure and be pure, as if your life (your eternal life) depended on it!

Beatitude #7:
"Blessed Are the Peacemakers, for They Shall Be Called the Sons of God"

Stream-Attitude: The "hawks" say war and violence are the solution; the "peaceniks" say there can be no just war. (Both are opposite errors.)

The previous section of this book discussed how all sorts of misunderstandings crept in after the Fifth Commandment, "Thou shalt not *murder*," morphed into "Thou shalt not *kill*." Well, now we come to what is probably the most widely misunderstood of the Beatitudes. All sorts of people (including Russian novelist Leo Tolstoy and Indian reformer Mahatma Gandhi), in many different times and places, have interpreted this as a mandate (calling) for pacifism—the view that any warfare at any time is always wrong.

But this is not what most Christians at most times have believed, or what Christ meant when he declared, "Blessed are the peacemakers." Why do so many people believe this refers to pacifism? At first glance it seems logical: people who make peace are blessed by God. So people who make war are cursed by God, right? Not necessarily. Let's try a little Logic 101 here. Say your mother tells your little brother or sister, "Blessed are those who clear the table." Would she really mean, "Cursed are those who eat food"? Don't think so. Making peace is an action blessed by God, but that doesn't necessarily mean all war is cursed by him. In fact, the Old Testament frequently represents God helping the Israelites in war against their enemies.

What about the New Testament? While it's true Christ told Peter to put away his sword and not fight against the soldiers who had come to arrest Christ (Matt. 26:52), there are two places where it's clear Christ does not condemn all violence or warfare. Christ himself committed a very justified act of violence against the money changers in the temple (Matt. 21:12–13), and, as we saw in the discussion on the Fifth Commandment, he praised the faith of the Roman Centurion, a soldier in the occupying army who came to Jesus in faith and asked him to heal his servant. If Christ really stood for pacifism, he would have condemned the centurion for being a soldier; instead, he strongly praised his faith (Luke 7:2–9).

What about the Body of Christ (the Church) in history? Hasn't it been teaching, healing, and sowing peace where there was violence and war? Yes. But it has also participated in wars that were justified. Which ones? Some are debatable, but there are at least four very clear examples: the Battle of the Milvian Bridge; the French war for independence from England (led by a teenaged girl named St. Joan of Arc); the Battle of Lepanto; and World War II. In the Battle of the Milvian Bridge, in 312 AD, the Roman emperor Constantine received a vision that he would, by the sign of the cross, conquer the army that wanted to destroy him. Nearly a thousand years later, St. Joan of Arc would respond to voices of angels and lead the French army to drive the British from France. Then, in 1571, Rome and the rest of Christian Europe were almost overrun by the Ottoman Turks, but Pope Pius V led the Church in a recitation of the Rosary and the Christian fleet stopped the larger Turkish invasion force in the Battle of Lepanto. The Church still celebrates the Feast of Our Lady, Queen of Victory (later changed to Our Lady of the Rosary) on October 7, the anniversary of the Battle of Lepanto. What about an example that's not from hundreds and hundreds of years ago? All right. How about Pope Pius XII during World War II? He received secret information from people in Germany who were working against Hitler and passed it along to the Allies; this shows he viewed the war against Hitler as a just war.

Then What *Does* It Mean?

So if this beatitude is not a call for pacifism, what does it call for? The answer is similar to something mentioned in our discussion of the Fifth Beatitude. It is your individual calling to be a peacemaker, not something you are supposed to wait for the government to do. We should not give in to the common tendency to deflate the force and power of the beatitudes by making them political causes for governments or other people and ignoring what they call us to in our own lives. Too many people say they want peace and justice politically and then ignore or mistreat their family members and neighbors—in other words, they live without peace and justice on the personal level. But that is precisely where Christ calls us to be peacemakers—on the personal and individual level. (And if some day you go on to make peace between whole countries, great; however, most people don't get placed into that kind of role.) So be a peacemaker here and now—today, in your home, at your school, or at your job.

How do you follow this teaching here and now? By making peace where there is hatred and division. When people get into disagreements that start to become serious, you might be the person who steps in and helps both sides come to an agreement. When two people get angry with each other, you might be the person who tells them to slow down and listen to each other and work out their problem. In order to make peace, you have to see some good in both parties and work with the good you see in both sides to come to a solution. With very few exceptions, most people prefer to get along with each other than to be at odds, divided or full of hatred. The job of a peacemaker is to tap into the desire on both sides to be at peace and get along. If you do that—if you help people be at peace with each other and get along—others will recognize God is working within you. Then you will be blessed by God and called a son (or daughter) of God.

On an international level, a number of people have been peacemakers between whole countries. Often in the Church's two-thousand-year history, popes have been peacemakers; they have ended some wars and prevented others from even starting. Pope Leo the Great once boldly met with the fierce barbarian, Attila the Hun, and convinced him not to attack Rome. Other popes have often played peacemaker between warring armies or countries. Benedict XVI tried unsuccessfully to establish peace just before and during World War I and then played a major part in establishing reconciliation in Europe afterwards. Other famous peacemakers are Mahatma Gandhi, Anwar Sadat, and Lech Walesa, the leader of the nonviolent Polish Solidarnosc movement that led to the peaceful ending of Soviet communist rule in Eastern Europe.

But even if you never become a peacemaker on a worldwide scale, you still can and should be a peacemaker in your family, your neighborhood, and wherever you study, work, play, eat, surf, bowl—

whatever it is you do to live, strive, and survive. Make what peace you can and you will be called a son (or daughter) of God.

Finally, the words of St. Francis of Assisi are worth reading and meditating upon. They are a beautiful prayer and a good example of what it means to be a peacemaker.

Lord, make me an instrument of Thy peace;

where there is hatred, let me sow love;

where there is injury, pardon;

where there is doubt, faith;

where there is despair, hope;

where there is darkness, light;

and where there is sadness, joy.

O Divine Master,

grant that I may not so much seek

to be consoled as to console;

to be understood, as to understand;

to be loved, as to love;

for it is in giving that we receive,

it is in pardoning that we are pardoned,

and it is in dying that we are born to Eternal Life.

Amen.

Beatitude #8:
"Blessed Are Those Who Are Persecuted for Righteousness' Sake, for Theirs Is the Kingdom of Heaven"

Stream-Attitude: Winning is the only thing. Tell 'em what they wanna hear. We don't need no righteousness, victory's all that matters here!

"My fellow Americans," beamed the candidate, "if ya just believe in me, if ya like what I'm sayin' and go to the polls and show it, we're gonna win, I tell ya! WIN!" Reg U. L'Dude waived at the cameras. His wife smiled her best "have-some-apple-pie" smile. The crowds cheered as the balloons went up. The crowds love a winner. L'Dude was on top of the world.

Unfortunately, like the guys who built the Tower of Babel, L'Dude felt close to the sky but far from the Guy in the Sky. Why? Because he was a crowd-pleaser instead of a God-pleaser. In his heart, he bowed not to God but to an idol: Gopo the Gargantuous (a distant cousin of Greedo the Gargantuan, mentioned in the discussion on the Tenth Commandment). Gopo (the God of Public Opinion) rewarded L'Dude with power, prestige, and a place in the media spotlight in exchange for his soul.

Meanwhile, a small Hispanic woman named Gloria was getting chewed out by the head nurse at the hospital where she worked in the rough part of town. Gloria had helped a pregnant woman decide against killing the child in her womb. She was told that if she continued to "inflict her morality on others," she would soon be seeking another position. She sought another position.

Gloria was the type of person Jesus was describing, while L'Dude was the exact opposite. Gloria was willing to endure persecution and even lose her job for the sake of righteousness; on the other hand, L'Dude only acted like he was interested in Christ and the Bible because he knew it would win the crowd's approval, but he never really got serious about following their teachings. He reduced all the rules of God to a simple message—"be nice and tolerant of other people"—without recognizing that Jesus also expressed his love through righteous anger, warnings, and hard words. Christ didn't care about public opinion. He cared about people. People like Gloria carry on his work today, while people like L'Dude do not, even though they like to say they do.

Successful versus Faithful

If we sincerely decide to follow Christ and put him before everything else in our lives, sooner or later we will endure the hatred and rejection of those around us. "If the world hates you," Jesus said, "know that it has hated Me before it hated you." (John 15:18) The last of the eight Great Beatitudes affirms the truth that we are blessed in God's sight if the world curses us because of our devotion to him—if we act like Gloria and not like L'Dude. Christ told us to expect persecution and even to welcome it because it sanctifies us in his service. If everybody loves us, we have to ask ourselves if we are really following Christ or are slipping under the influence of Gopo the Gargantuous.

The thing about Gopo is that the God of Public Opinion sometimes casts his spell over us even when we think we're following Christ. If being liked and being popular ever starts to matter more to you than following God's call, you know you're starting to fall under the influence of Gopo. We all sometimes start to bow to him in various ways. When we're with our friends and someone ridicules our beliefs, aren't there times when we remain silent or even laugh along when we should speak the truth? Haven't we all done stupid things because we wanted to fit in or be thought of as cool or hip? When Gopo suddenly focuses the Crowd of Cool People on us, don't we sometimes say, like St. Peter, "No way, man, I don't even know the dude!" Then the cock crows again. Maybe it's the third time, or maybe the third hundredth.

Take a Stand, Man

But St. Peter made a comeback, and so should we. Our comeback may not rock the world's boat so much as St. Peter's did (he became the Rock on which the Church was built). But we can still make a comeback and hold firm to our Lord, just as St. Peter did, even to the point of suffering execution for Christ's sake. As we grow in strength and build up our fortitude (inner strength, which is one of the virtues), we learn to stand up to Gopo and refuse to bow to the strong narcotic of public opinion. We learn to withstand the rejection of others: because we won't do drugs or participate in cruel gossip about other people, or because we save sex for marriage, or go to church regularly, or put Christ first in any of the other areas of our life where the crowd would rather have us put him second, or third, fourth, fifth, or twentieth. We may not always win in the eyes of the world, but we grow in blessedness and the happiness the world can never know, give, or take away. Mother Teresa pointed out that we are not called to be successful; we are called to be faithful. If God rewards us with success, as he did Mother Teresa's Missionaries of Charity, that's fine, but success shouldn't be our priority; faithfulness and righteousness should be.

All who take a stand for what is good, true, and right are blessed by God, even if they are not professing Christians. As Bishop Fulton Sheen once pointed out, God has many that the Church does not have, and the Church has many that God does not have. However, if we endure persecution because we belong to Christ, we are especially blessed by God. Nobody likes to be persecuted, but if it happens to you because you stood up for Christ, you can take comfort in the words of Jesus that he is drawing you closer to himself even through the bad behavior of others. St. Thomas More wrote the following prayer, "Almighty God have mercy ... on all that bear me evil will, and would me harm, and their faults and mine together ... and make us saved souls in heaven together where we may ever live and love together with thee and they blessed saints." In another work, St. Thomas mentioned that the brothers of Joseph (in the Old Testament story of Joseph and the Coat of Many Colors in Genesis, Ch. 37) could not have done him as much good by kindness as they did with their malice and hatred. In other words, God has plans for you and the hatred of others may actually help you grow closer to him and end up in a better place. So, even if it hurts to be on the outside, rejected, put down, or ridiculed because you belong to Christ, rejoice and be glad. God has plans for your that go way beyond the plans of cool people who act *uncool* toward you because you put God, not coolness (or political correctness or hipness), first.

Introduction to the Virtues

Pope Benedict XVI recently pointed out that the problem with a lot of biblical scholarship today is that it focuses exclusively on the Bible while ignoring the "living tradition of the whole Church." Starting in the early 1500s (with the former Catholic monk, Martin Luther), the idea of *sola scriptura*, or that the Bible alone should be the sole authority for Christian teaching, became popular among many former Catholics—now calling themselves Protestants. The problem with this approach, as the former Presbyterian minister, Scott Hahn, once pointed out, is that it is not found in the Bible! Not only that, but the Bible actually says the exact opposite (for example, 2 Thess. 2:15, 3:6), and the exact opposite was taught by the early Church fathers. St. Augustine, for example, wrote, "I would put no faith in the Gospels unless the authority of the Catholic Church directed me to do so." In other words, this fifth century theologian, respected by both Catholic and Protestant thinkers today, took a clear position *against* the idea of *sola scriptura*. What a lot of people (including Catholics) seem to forget nowadays is that the Catholic Church put the Bible together, and the Church made decisions about which books belonged in the Bible and which ones (like the Gnostic gospels) did not. It's important to keep these things in mind as we turn to the virtues.

Unlike the Commandments and the Beatitudes, the first four virtues do not come directly from the Bible. They actually come from ancient Greek philosophers. They are examples of truths from outside the Bible that were adopted by the Church and became part of Church teaching. Two of the earliest Church fathers to write about them were St. Ambrose and St. Augustine; several centuries later, during the Middle Ages, St. Thomas Aquinas incorporated the virtues into his philosophy, which many people consider the semiofficial philosophy of the Catholic Church. Today, the virtues can be found in the Catechism of the Catholic Church.

The first four virtues are called the cardinal virtues for reasons that are not widely understood nowadays. The name did not originate with the St. Louis Cardinals or the birds that feed from your dad's backyard bird feeder. And the name has nothing to do with the Church officials who wear those red hats. The word *cardinal* comes from the Latin word *cardo,* which means hinge. Before you get unhinged trying to understand this, let's clarify something. The first four virtues are considered the hinges of the moral life. Prudence, fortitude, temperance, and justice help people live good (even if not perfect) lives, even without the light of Christian revelation.

However, once your moral door is hinged onto those four virtues, you're ready for the three higher virtues, which come from the light of God's self-revelation and so are called the theological virtues: faith, hope, and love. These virtues are found in both the Old and New Testaments, starting with the description of Jacob's ladder in Genesis and mentioned again in St. Paul's Epistle to the Corinthians—"So faith, hope, and love abide, these three: and the greatest of these is love" (1 Cor. 13:13). St. Paul's point is that the virtues are all wonderful gifts, but they are useless unless crowned with love. Let's compare them to a well-built car: it can get you to any destination quickly and efficiently. But if you drive it to the wrong places, the car only helps you do wrong things. In the same way, there have been terrible dictators who had the virtues of prudence and temperance, and there have been cruel and heartless people who had some degree of faith and hope, but unless love is there, all the other virtues in the world won't bring a person to God. As St. Paul put it, "If I speak in tongues of men and of angels, but have not love, I am a noisy gong and a clanging cymbal. And if I have prophetic powers, and understand all mysteries and all knowledge, and if I have all faith, so as to remove mountains, but have not love, I am nothing" (1 Cor. 13:1–2).

For that reason, the order of the virtues in the following pages starts with the cardinal virtues and ends with the greatest virtue of them all—the crown of love. This saves the best for last. There's also an artistic unity between the First Commandment and the virtue of love. God, who is Love, made clear to Moses and the Israelites that they should put him first above any other gods. The first commandment was to love God first. The virtue of love also originates with God and is expressed toward our fellow human beings. All the commandments, beatitudes, and virtues are about loving God first and then loving others as ourselves. And since there are a million and one ways to love others (or not), the virtues (and all the other God Rules) show us how it's done in our everyday lives.

Virtue #1:
Prudence

The Virtue: *Prudence is a tendency to judge well, to follow good advice, and to choose wisely.*

The Hurt-You: *Do-dance is an impulsive dance of "monkey see, monkey do" by someone who does dumb things and will not stop, look, and listen to wisdom.*

Kia and Dia, twin sisters, had established a reputation for rushing into things—especially dangerous, mind-altering, or immoral things. When the kids at school wanted to become "Maxie-Zombie-Faced Waste-oids," they knew who to hang out with. When one of the guys wanted a quick, easy "relationship," he would give Kia or Dia a call. One night, the twins were at a party, even though they had a ton of homework due the next morning. Dave the Drunk swaggered up to them. "So, how are you dabes boin'?" he drawled.

Kia laughed and turned to her sister. "You don't think Dave's been drinkin' again, do you?" she asked and laughed some more.

Dia looked Dave over and asked, "So, how many drinks have you had, Dave?"

Dave scratched his head and grinned. "Just a bew feers …"

Kia laughed again. "Is that all?

Dave continued, "—and a couple wine coolers … and … and …" His voice trailed off as he became absorbed in deep thought, or something like it.

Kia and Dia laughed again, as Dave suddenly remembered what he wanted to tell them. "Oh, yeah!" he said. "Look, there's a rager at Steggy's. His parents are in Mexico. I'm about to drive up there in my pickup. Wanna go?"

De Do-Dance

Kia and Dia had to learn prudence and they had to learn it fast. They had to slow down, stop, think, and listen. Kia (Know-It-All) and Dia (Do-It-All) were about to get a crash course in imprudent choices. They were headed for a serious accident, AIDS, suicide, or, at least, a lifetime of regret and low self-esteem.

Luckily, their guardian angels decided just in time to dial 1-800-PRU-DENT. Kia felt a strange feeling inside and uttered a statement that surprised Dia and even herself. "I don't know. Maybe we shouldn't ride with Dave while he's trashed."

Dia had followed her sister along the path to many unwise actions, but this time, she also felt an unusual feeling. She decided to listen to her sister again—this time in the *right* direction. She decided she would do the right thing, which in this case (like many cases) was to refrain from doing the wrong thing. She said, "I think Kia's right. Sorry, Dave, we're not gonna do it."

Dave frowned and said, "All right, whatever. So you're just gonna be a couple prudes tonight, huh?" He turned around and stumbled toward the door, left the party, and got into his four-by-fool. He started the engine and drove off into the darkness. The next day, Kia and Dia discovered Dave had totaled his pickup, and anyone in the back would have been toast. They had stopped the Do-Dance just in time.

What Is Prudence?

Prudence is a humble virtue. It's not about acting before you think; it's about thinking before you act. It takes humility to admit you don't know all the answers and to seek the advice of others who know more than you. It might seem more fun to listen to cool people who pressure you into things you know are wrong, but a prudent person listens to his own conscience, the teachings of Scripture and the Church, and adults who truly know how to have a long and happy life. Up until the night Kia and Dia almost lost their lives, they almost never practiced prudence. They ignored the advice of their parents and teachers and never stopped to reflect about anything. They had no concept of self-control.

But deep down, Kia and Dia both knew the Do-Dance wasn't making them happy. They felt emptiness inside because the more they did everything they felt like doing the less they felt fulfilled and happy. Kia wasn't known for reading a lot, but she found an answer one day when she happened to read a statement of St. Augustine: "Our hearts are restless, until they rest in Thee." As time passed, she and her evil twin grew out of their empty lives and discovered prudence. They sensed it was a better and more fulfilling way to live.

Prude or Rude?

Back in the early '90s, comedian Dana Carvey made a name for himself imitating President George H.W. Bush (the first President Bush) on *Saturday Night Live* using the signature phrase, "Wouldn't be prudent!" A number of teen comedies show characters who use the word *prude* to describe fellow teens who refuse sex or drugs. The concept of prudence is often mocked and put down in popular culture. Maybe you've heard people at your school say, "Don't be such a prude!" The word doesn't sound very appealing, sort of a cross between prune and rude. It's not a label a lot of teens want.

Prude is the term often used to bully or pressure people into doing something they know is wrong. It's word that has been used to cheat young girls out of their virginity and people of both genders out of their innocence with regards to smoking or underage drinking. When people say, "I don't want to be a prude!" they are usually responding out of insecurity or fear of being rejected instead of calm, reflective, prayerful judgment. But if being called a prude is the punishment for acting with prudence, then we should get over our shame about the label. No one has ever ruined his life by thinking clearly and deciding not to do something that's wrong; but a lot of people have ruined their lives by failing to consider the consequences of their actions and doing something stupid. Once someone decides it is more important to obey the cool people than to be wise and virtuous, he is on the path to destruction, unhappiness, grief, and regret.

Prudence is a virtue that leads to success and happiness. Instead of doing what the crowd pressures us into, we should seek the friendship and advice of those who set a good example and are rooted in solid faith and moral values. Maybe it's a parent, a priest, a teacher, or an older sister or brother; maybe it's the examples in the Bible or those whose biographies can be found in a book on the lives of the saints. We exercise prudence when we seek good advice and follow it.

Just like with our physical bodies, the more we exercise it, the stronger it becomes. And the stronger it becomes, the happier we become; the humility and self-control of a temperate person lead to the freedom and happiness we all desire and help him become a powerful witness to friends and neighbors.

Virtue #2:
Fortitude

The Virtue: *Fortitude is inner strength or courage. It means holding to what is right without letting danger, peer pressure, or any other difficulty cause you to change or back down.*

The Hurt-You: *Forget-it-dude is the habit of giving up on what one believes due to fear of discomfort or rejection for doing what's right or refusing to do what's wrong.*

Elmer Fugeddaboudit (a distant relative of Elmer Fudd) was cruising with his buddies, driving around late at night to no place in particular.

"Hey," yelled one of the dorks, "let's go steal some booze from that liquor store!" The others laughed. But then the laughing stopped.

"We could, you know …" said another voice.

Another highly original voice added, "Yeah!"

Soon there were four lowlife dudes walking up to the liquor store to steal some beer. The plan was for Elmer to distract the clerk while his friends grabbed a few six packs and quietly headed out the door.

"Hey, Abu!" Elmer said to the clerk with a smile. "How much for those lottery tickets, buddy?"

"My name's not Abu, man, it's Abe … and I'll have to check."

While Abe checked the price, Elmer's friends acted fast. They grabbed a few six packs, hid them under their coats, and headed for the door. They got away clean, or so they thought. Abe's wife happened to be watching the action on the security camera in the back room.

Meanwhile, Elmer and his buddies were back on the road—cruising, drinking, and driving dangerously. For a moment, Elmer doubted he should be doing what he was doing. He thought about pulling over or driving home to sober up. Then a loud voice interrupted his thoughts, "Hey, Elmo! Let's race that motorcycle, man!"

Without thinking, Elmer gunned the engine and the car picked up speed. Soon afterward, he saw police lights flashing in his rearview mirror. You can guess what happened next. Elmer and his loser friends were charged with drunk driving, underage drinking, and theft. All of this could have been avoided if Elmer had the fortitude to tell his friends no.

Fortitude for Teens/Adults

For many teens, the virtue of fortitude means the ability to say no to peer pressure. Elmer did whatever his buddies told him to, and his lack of fortitude landed him in jail. After all, he was driving the car; he could have refused to pull up at the liquor store, cover for his friends' crime, drink and drive, or speed after the motorcycle. He could have, but he didn't. When he needed to do the right thing, his response—like his last name—was fugeddaboudit. If you have fortitude, nobody can pressure you into doing something you know is wrong, whether it's stealing, smoking, drinking, drugs, sex, cheating, spreading lies, or anything else your conscience pulls you away from. We all face situations where everyone around us is acting a certain way, and we know in our hearts the way they're acting is not good. Many people go along with the crowd because they're afraid to stand out or appear as if they are not with it. A person with fortitude, however, does not give in to that fear; he is man (or woman) enough to stand on his own. And if the cool people put him down or reject him, he's tough enough to take it. His inner strength makes him like a rock under the ocean's waves: no matter how forcefully they wash against it, it won't budge. And if he loses some friends, he realizes he doesn't need losers for friends; there are always more people who can become friends.

In the adult world, fortitude sometimes involves saying no to peers, but it also might mean taking an unpopular stand, refusing to follow a company or government policy that is wrong, or getting on the bad side of a boss who wants you to do something you know is not right. A person with fortitude has the courage and integrity to stick to the truth, do the right thing, and accept the consequences. Unlike the world of childhood, the adult world often punishes good deeds. But a man or woman of fortitude doesn't let the consequences of doing the right thing stop him from doing them.

An outstanding example of someone with great fortitude is St. Thomas More. (For the full story, check out the film *A Man for All*

Seasons, which won six Academy Awards in 1966.) King Henry VIII was one of the most feared and hot-tempered tyrants in all of history. Thomas More was one of the most respected authors and government officials of the day precisely because of his commitment to what was right and true. When King Henry decided to defy the Church, divorce his queen, and marry his mistress, More refused to condone it even when everyone else did. When all eyes were watching to see if he would voice his approval, he remained silent. King Henry knew of Thomas More's reputation for honesty and intelligence and tried in all sorts of ways to change More's mind. He had More imprisoned, relentlessly questioned, and pressured by friends and family members. Eventually More was put on trial and a kangaroo court pronounced him guilty. One of the most powerful moments in *A Man for All Seasons* is when More confronts Richard Rich, who has just given the court the false evidence it needed to sentence More to death. After finding out Rich had been appointed to a position in the realm of Wales, More questions him: "Why Richard, it profits a man nothing to give his soul for the whole world, but for Wales?" (The reference is to Matt. 16:26.) More showed outstanding fortitude because he had the courage to stand for what was right, even if it cost him his life—and it did. King Henry had him executed, along with St. John Fisher and hundreds of faithful Catholics who refused to renounce their loyalty to the Church of Rome instead of joining King Henry's new and improved Church of England.

Who were others who have showed great fortitude? Dietrich Bonhoeffer and Franz Jagerstatter were German citizens who opposed Hitler, even though it cost them their lives. Bonhoeffer was a Lutheran pastor who fearlessly preached against the Nazi regime. He was executed in 1945. Jagerstatter was a young German farmer who refused to serve in Hitler's army because of his religious convictions, which were rooted in his Catholic faith. He was also arrested and executed in 1943. In one of his last letters, Jagerstatter wrote, "Just as the man who thinks only of this world does everything possible to make life here easier and better, so must we, too, who believe in the eternal Kingdom, risk everything in order to receive a great reward there." Jagerstatter was beatified (declared Blessed) by the Catholic Church in 2007. It was the Church's way of voicing its conviction that Jagerstatter is receiving the great reward of which he wrote, a reward he now shares with Bonheoffer and countless other brave souls who had the fortitude to stand for what was right in the face of tyranny, threats, murder, and oppression.

Fortitude for You, Dude

So the sixty-four-dollar question is: will you ever need the kind of fortitude shown by Thomas More, Dietrich Bonhoeffer, and Franz Jagerstatter? Only God knows. The odds are against it, but if you had asked these men during their youth if they thought it likely they would face the kind of trials they faced, they certainly would have said no. Whether your trials are great or small, fortitude helps you endure the hardships that will come, one way or another, whenever you choose to defy the crowd and live a godly life.

But fortitude does not simply help us withstand peer pressure; it also helps us have courage and strength when doing the right thing may involve physical danger or discomfort. Another example of great fortitude was Fifth Officer Harold Lowe, a junior officer aboard the Titanic the night it hit an iceberg and sank (April 14, 1912). There weren't enough lifeboats for everyone on board, so most passengers did not survive the sinking. After the ship sank completely, many passengers were stranded in the freezing water. Most of the lifeboats did not return to save them because the people in the boats were afraid they would be overwhelmed with swimmers trying to get aboard. Only one boat returned to pull survivors out of the water, and it was commanded by Lowe. Most of the survivors in the water had already died from the freezing temperatures, but Lowe's boat managed to save three who were still alive. Because of this, Lowe is probably the greatest hero of that terrible tragedy; he had the fortitude to risk himself and his boat to do the right thing. The possibility of criticism, pressure, or physical danger did not stop him from doing what he knew was right—trying to save innocent lives.

The Wrap

Fortitude is what you need to persevere in being and becoming the good man or woman God intends you to be. If you have it, no one and nothing can stop you from doing the right thing: no cool people, no tyrant bosses, no physical danger, and no threats, bullying, or peer pressure. By holding firm and having the courage to withstand everything around you that may turn you from what's right, you grow into a rock or anchor who will be a good example to others and help them do the same. When you have the opportunity to resist something bad, you won't respond to the pull of your conscience by saying, like Elmer, "Forget about it, dude!" Instead, you'll respond with the conviction of fortitude. As the character Edmond Dantes (in the 2002 film *The Count of Monte Cristo*) told his young friend, Albert, on his sixteenth birthday, "Life is a storm, my young friend. You will bask in the sunlight one moment, and be shattered on the rocks the next. What makes you a man is what you do when that storm comes. You must look into that storm and shout as you did ... Do your worst, for I will do mine!"

Virtue #3:
Temperance

The Virtue: Temperance is the habit of self-control that keeps us from becoming addicted to drugs, drinking, sex, power, or any passion that can destroy our freedom and peace of mind.

The Hurt-You: Pleasurance is the view that says, "If it feels good, do it" without caring about the consequences, other people, or God.

Dave D. Structo (a.k.a. "Dave the Drunk") comes whipping around this curve in his four-by-fool. He's drunk, he's speeding, and he's angry. Dave is on his way from one party to another, and it's way too late on a Saturday night. His reactions are slow because he's plastered, and he's angry because he's just been turned down by the two girls who never turn any guy down for anything—or so he thought. "Kia and Dia are sooooo stuck up!" he says to himself, pounding his fist on the dashboard and turning up the "music" on his Ghetto-blast woofers. "They're just a couple of prudes, anyway! Who needs 'em?" He loses himself in a rap song that degrades women, promotes violence, and uses over 100 curse words in less than three minutes.

Suddenly, a fluffy white cat runs out in front of his pickup as he goes around the turn. Dave turns the wheel hard to the left and barely misses the cat. But he doesn't miss the guard rail. He slams on his brakes, but it's too late. *WHAM!* Down the hill he goes: *WUMP-DE-WUMP-DE-WUMP-DE-WUMP!* Dave's lucky. Someone calls 911 right away and the paramedics are on the scene in minutes. He's still breathing. They get him into an ambulance and to a hospital in time to save his life. Years later, he has only one question: who called 911 so quickly? He was alone when the accident happened, so he figures it must have been the cat ...

Dave was still in therapy a year after the accident, learning to walk again. Through all his pain and difficulty, he finally learned what he should have found out long before. The therapy group Dave attends calls it self-control or self-discipline—or sometimes "knowing when to quit." But whether they realize it or not, it's something the Church has taught for centuries: the virtue of temperance. By the way, nobody calls him Dave the Drunk anymore; now they just call him Dave de De-Tox Dude.

Temper, Temperance

The word *temperance* comes from the Latin word *temporare*, which means to regulate and mix properly. We're not talking about a good bartender; in fact, temperance has more to do with *not* mixing too many drinks. When a metal worker mixes melted metals, he is *tempering* the metal so it has the desired qualities. We also say the metal has a *temper* that can be weakened by extreme heat or cold, pressure, or stress. In a sense, you could say that under extreme stress, metal, like people, can lose its temper.

"No way, dude, you mean like a crowbar could lose its temper? Like, I'd hate to be around when that happens!" Actually, it sounds like a joke, but that's where we get the expression "to lose your temper." Just as every piece of metal has its own proper temper or personality (metality?), each person has a proper mixture of feelings, thoughts, and emotions, and under extreme stress, every person can lose his original, God-given temper.

Most people in today's society think of temper as referring to anger only. But its original meaning had to do with more than that; it meant a proper mixture of and control over all feelings and desires. As long as you are practicing temperance, your feelings and desires don't take control of you; rather, you control them. A temperate person is a free person; an intemperate person is a slave to his passions. If you practice temperance, you can control not just anger, but also sexual attraction, jealousy, greed, or the desire to eat, drink, smoke, or play video games. A person who lacks temperance, like Dave before his accident, is a sitting duck—ready to be enslaved by whatever feeling or desire comes along. So he becomes an addict to drink, anger, or lust, and he's a prime candidate for some form of self-destruction. Without temperance, you can become just like a DDS who can end up DOA (a Dave D. Structo who ends up dead on arrival.)

Temperance versus Pleasurance

Ever since the '60s, popular culture in America has been like one big "pleasure-olatry." Millions of people followed entertainers and popular icons who lived (and died) by the "if it feels good, do it" philosophy. This nice-sounding idea caught on like wildfire and soon destroyed the lives of singers like Jim Morrison, Janis Joplin, and Jimi Hendrix. Entertainers like John Belushi and Chris Farley suffered the same fate. You could probably name dozens more. Millions still follow this deadly mentality. Pope John Paul II wasn't kidding when he spoke about the Culture of Death (and how we need to counter it by building a Culture of Life). Many people who were intemperate in their youth have spent long, hard years trying to reconstruct their lives without the drugs, alcohol, or promiscuous sex that characterized their younger days. A popular song from the '80s contained the lyrics, "I used to be a renegade, I used to fool around / But I couldn't take the punishment and had to settle down" (from "Hip to be Square," by Huey Lewis and the News).

We can learn from the examples all around us. If the pursuit of happiness becomes the intemperate pursuit of pleasurance, we won't be truly happy and fulfilled. Dave the Drunk had to learn the hard way that pleasurance ends up killing pleasure. Isn't it funny how, sometimes, the harder you pursue something, the more you push it away? A drug addict or alcoholic—or former addict—who's honest will admit he no longer enjoys the drinking or drugs to which he has become addicted; he just doesn't know how to quit. He began seeking pleasure and ended up losing even the pleasure the drug or alcohol used to give him. He doesn't continue because he enjoys it but because he has lost his freedom to take it or leave it and has fallen into a sorry state where he *needs* it.

Real happiness is found through moderate—that is, *temperate*—enjoyment of all the good and wholesome pleasures God gives us. The only way we can enjoy life's pleasures and not fall into a form of enslavement is to enjoy them without going overboard. Despite what we're conditioned to think, singer Bobby McFerrin had it right when he wrote his song, "Simple Pleasures Are the Best."

Virtue #4:
Justice

The Virtue: *Justice is the habit of respecting the rights and dignity of all others and, more generally, fair play between persons and groups in a community.*

The Hurt-You: *Just-us is a close-minded tendency to see all problems and issues in terms of how they affect just one racial, economic, gender, or ethnic group: mine.*

Right in the middle of recess, Billy the Bully came up behind Justin Thyme and smashed a Ding Dong all over Justin's shirt. He laughed like a maniac and ran across the yard. Justin took off after him. A few of Billy's lieutenants were about to gang up on Justin when Sister Always Fairly arrived on the scene. "Both of you young men are in big trouble!" she said, with her "now you're busted" scowl. "B-b-but, Sister!" Justin screamed. "That's not fair! Billy started it! See!" He turned and showed her the chocolate cake and creme filling smeared all over his back. Sister Always Fairly reconsidered. She grabbed Billy's ear and said, "Billeeeee, you're comin' with me." As Justin watched Billy being marched to the office, he sat down and smiled. "At last," he said, "Justin Thyme just got justice, and just in time ..."

A lot of us may not have a clear concept of the virtue of justice, but we sure know what it feels like to be treated unjustly. If you've ever told a teacher or parent, "That's not fair!" you were complaining about a lack of justice, or at least what you thought was a lack of justice. In the example above, Sister Always Fairly served justice by punishing only the guilty. But there are many cases where justice does not prevail. What happens then?

In a famous statement, Pope Paul VI once said, "If you want peace, work for justice." Years later, in 1992, many demonstrators chanted, "No justice, no peace," in response to the release of police officers videotaped beating Rodney King. There is a connection between justice and peace in a community. Have you noticed some teachers who show favoritism and act unfairly tend to have unruly classes, while other teachers who try to be fair toward all students generally have more order and cooperation? People are at peace with each other if they feel their rights and dignity are respected. If they receive injustice, they react. Countless demonstrations, strikes, and wars have started because of a real or perceived lack of justice.

Justice *Is* for All (or It's Not Justice)

We have a clear idea how injustice affects us. We know all people tend to react when they suffer from it, which is only natural. But to really understand justice, we have to look at the whole picture, beyond injustice that affects us directly. Gradually, as Justin Thyme grows older, he has to be just and work for justice even when an injustice doesn't involve him directly in order to acquire the virtue of justice. As the great civil rights leader Martin Luther King, Jr. once said, "Injustice anywhere is a threat to justice everywhere." If you truly acquire the virtue of justice, then you are concerned about the rights and dignity of *all* people, not just those of your own racial, ethnic, age, or gender group. If a person's concern for justice stops after his own group gets empowerment, then he does not really have the virtue. Basically, when he says justice, he really means "just us."

Justice is not simply giving power to groups that have been victimized. In fact, true justice is not a matter of power at all, except perhaps how to limit the power strong, influential groups have to oppress smaller, weaker ones. Justice has more to do with fair play and equality between *all* persons, rich or poor, male or female, Jew or Christian, black or white, American or foreign, born or unborn. Because all people—even those who are poor, ugly, uneducated, can't surf, or cheer for the Oakland Raiders—still are made in the image and likeness of the living God. So the most lowly, ignorant street person has an importance and dignity equal to the most idolized, paparazzi-followed, rich and famous celebrity or powerful politician. If we truly understand that all persons have equal worth and dignity, it will show in how we interact with others.

These are some points of reflection regarding justice and injustice.

- **Racial Justice:** The American people have come a long way in their attempts to establish a racially just society. Up until the election of President Lincoln in 1860, slavery was a normal economic practice in many parts of our country. Lincoln's abolitionist sympathies were well-known and inspired the South to declare war. A deeply spiritual and Bible-believing man, Lincoln believed it was God's will that slaves be liberated. After a long and bloody war, slavery was finally abolished. But institutionalized racism continued until the 1960s, when nonviolent protesters under the leadership of Dr. Martin Luther King, Jr., another deeply religious man, brought an end to all legal discrimination based on race. As it stands now, racial injustice persists in subtle ways even though racism is no longer a declared public practice. Police officers, civil officials, and corporations still sometimes give special or unusually bad treatment based on race. And sometimes reverse racism is found in the expressions of some rap artists and social activists. While we've achieved a lot, we still have a long way to go.

- **Gender Justice:** This is a hot issue that sometimes gets people really steamed up. For years, women were often treated unjustly in the realms of jobs and higher education. The recent advancement of women in these areas is also an advancement of justice. The hot topic is this: are *all* cases where men and women are treated differently cases of injustice? When Christians discuss this issue, St. Paul is often quoted, "You are all the same in Christ, Jew or Gentile, male or female, servant or free no more." So we all have equal worth and dignity in Christ. But Paul also said we all have different gifts and callings to exercise in Christ; we are many parts, we are all one body. God created two sexes, and both have their own special gifts and callings. While justice is advanced when women are treated equally in careers and higher education, there are two areas where allowing for gender differences is not injustice—in the Church and in the family. Both women and men have special gifts to bring to these areas, and the real injustice is to say that the calling of women lacks dignity and worth unless it is exactly the same as that of men. Some people claim that requiring one man and one woman for a valid Sacrament of Matrimony or reserving priestly ordination for males are injustices against women. But the opposite is true: the complainers are actually doing an injustice to women by saying women don't have worth and dignity unless they imitate and take the place of men.

- **Justice of Ages:** Related to gender justice is what we might call justice of ages. Since real justice sees the equal worth of *all* humans, both those who are very old and those who are very, very young (still inside their mothers' wombs) need to be respected and protected. Even if a human being can't do anything, even if he's very old or not born yet, he still has worth and dignity because God created him and loves him. Abortion and euthanasia are injustices because they violate the worth and dignity of those who are the smallest and most defenseless, or else those who are the most weakened. Christians should oppose those who publicly voice their approval of abortion or euthanasia even if they hold the most powerful offices in our government. Abortion, especially, is the most flagrant of injustices because it is a legally protected violence against women *and* children.

- **Justice in Your Life:** Besides justice as a social virtue—just in case you're looking at the above paragraphs and saying, "Yeah, yeah, but what's that got to do with my everyday life?"—it also has practical applications for you as an individual. It means that when you play in a game, you play fair; if you win, you don't ridicule the loser; and if you lose, you congratulate the winner. It means not cutting in the lunch line because the little geeky guy in front of you has just as much of a right to get his lunch as you do. It means you don't cheat on a test; if you get an *A* it's because you earned it, and if you deserve an *F* you take it instead of devaluing the grades of others who earned their grades honestly.

So whether you're a basket weaver in Tibet, a Venezuelan llama tender, a kangaroo catcher from Australia, or a surfer from Kansas (?), remember that all people have equal worth and dignity. The truer we are to this principle the more we will treat people as they truly are: each equally—in over five billion different and fascinating ways—the image and likeness of God.

Virtue #5:
Faith

The Virtue: *Faith is the habit of maintaining beliefs you have accepted as true, day to day, month to month, year to year, leading to habitual resignation to God's will.*

The Hurt-You: *Drift from beliefs you have once accepted as true, leading to lack of confidence in God, leading to worry and anxiety about the future.*

Ann Xiety was lying in bed wide awake. She was worrying on and on about everything that could go wrong in her life. What if the other students at school rejected her? What if her boyfriend, Warren Worrier, decided to leave her? What if she didn't do well on her English test? What if she lost her job? The constant worrying robbed Ann of inner peace, because she had not yet learned the virtue of faith in God, which reduces or eliminates our anxiety about the future, and helps us eliminate the natural human tendency to think everything depends on *us*, rather than on God.

When Christians talk about the virtue of faith, they mean the habit of maintaining belief in the truths revealed in the Bible and preserved by the body of Christian believers since the time of Christ. We are given the gift of faith at our baptism, but we have the virtue of faith only if we keep it and preserve it through the trials and tribulations (all the ups and downs) of life. Faith is a gift given to us by God's grace, but like any other freely given gift it can be kept or thrown away. The expression "keep the faith!" shows that maintaining faith through time is an act of the will; it's something we do in cooperation with God's grace. Since faith is something not just given once but chosen again and again, it is considered a virtue. St. Paul recognized this when he encouraged the Thessalonians to "hold firm to the traditions which you were taught by us" (2 Thess. 2:15) and the Philippians to "work out your own salvation with fear and trembling" (Phil. 2:12).

Faith of the Mind and of the Heart

There are two kinds of faith, and they work hand in hand—faith of the mind and faith of the heart. Faith of the mind is the intellectual acceptance of the truths revealed in the Bible and Church teaching, including the creeds and dogmas of the Church. Generally, most people are taught these things as children and then decide whether they will keep them and continue to live by them when they become adults. If you have the virtue of faith, you continue on. Instead of just accepting them in your mind once, you grow in them and renew them in your day-to-day life. Catholics are required to attend Mass every Sunday in part to help them to remember and strengthen their commitment to the truths of faith that they accepted once but need to make an effort to maintain. It can be difficult to maintain faith with all the obligations, commitments, cares, and concerns that fill our daily lives. All of those things, along with our human weakness, make it necessary that at least once a week we join with an assembly of our fellow believers to reaffirm our faith and encounter our Lord in the most holy Sacrament. But to really maintain faith, Sunday Mass once a week is not enough. We also need to take time to pray each day and study the Bible and spiritual writings as often as we can. That is how we maintain faith of the mind.

We also maintain faith of the mind by questioning those who try to lead us away from our faith. There are several best-selling books by atheist authors (like Richard Dawkins and Christopher Hitchens) who use their own versions of science, philosophy, or history to attack faith in God. There are also many people who teach classes in schools, colleges, and universities and present slanted versions of Church history, science, or philosophy in order to undermine Christian faith in general and Catholic faith in particular. We maintain faith of the mind by making an effort to find answers to those who try to attack and explain away the faith of our fathers. If we have doubts because of attacks on faith from today's colleges and universities, a great author to read is the former atheist, and professor at Oxford and Cambridge universities, C. S. Lewis. If we have doubts because of attacks against the Church from fundamentalist "Bible" Christians, we can turn to the Web site www.catholicanswers.com. For every attack against our faith, there is a good answer; we just need to make an effort to find it. To maintain faith of the mind, we need to remember the advice of St.

Peter: "Always be prepared to make a defense to anyone who calls you to account for the hope that is in you" (1 Pet. 3:15).

Faith of the heart has to do with feelings toward God and how much you trust in him and his plan for your life. Jesus made it crystal clear: he wants us to have complete trust and confidence in Him. This means not just an intellectual assent of our minds but a heartfelt and worry-free confidence in God. "Therefore I tell you, do not be anxious about your life, what you shall eat or what you shall drink, nor about your body, what you shall put on. Is not life more than food, and the body more than clothing? Look at the birds of the air: they neither sow nor reap nor gather into barns, and yet your heavenly Father feeds them. Are you not of more value than they?" (Matt. 6:25–26). Jesus also pointed out how the Father knows everything about us—even the number of hairs on our heads—so we have no reason to hold back our faith and trust. Even though human weakness, and the influence of the world and the Prince of this World, may try to sway us from the complete trust and abandonment to his will to which he calls us, the virtue of faith helps us rebuild and maintain the attitude that keeps us returning to God and the sincere prayer of "thy will be done." If we have the virtue of faith not only in our minds but in our hearts, those words are not just words; rather, they are a sincere and heartfelt way of life that no amount of suffering, problems, or difficulties can shake.

If we have the virtue of faith, we will not allow ourselves to get caught up in worries about the future. We make plans for the future, but that's all. Once the planning is done, we don't worry and agonize about the things that could go wrong; we leave it in God's hands. Worry and anxiety have no place in the heart of a faithful Christian. We may have concern about things from time to time, but we don't worry. The difference between concern and worry is that one is active while the other is passive (and useless). *Concern* is something that motivates you to action; if there's a problem, you do something about it, even if the only thing you can do is pray. On the other hand, *worry* is passive and inactive; you let it eat away at you, and your anxiety and fears keep you from doing anything. Worry and anxiety are the products of lack of faith, and they lead to stress and health problems as well. Once again, we see how following the instructions of the Designer of the human machine leads to long and happy usage; ignoring those instructions causes it to get damaged or broken.

A person with the virtue of faith is happy and carefree; he is not weighed down by the worries, stress, and anxiety of those who lack faith. His life is not weighed down with the cares of this world because it is shaped by Christ's principle that "the truth shall set you free" (John 8:32). His mind is not constantly imagining the thousands of ways things could go wrong. Instead, he has a natural confidence in God to order and provide for his life. When the storms of life come, he looks to Jesus—as Peter did when he walked on the water—to lift him up and carry him through. And he knows even bad things will work out for the better. As St. Paul expressed it, "We know that in everything God works for the good" (Rom. 8:28); later, the Apostle concludes, "For I am sure that neither death, nor life, nor angels, nor principalities, nor things present, nor things to come, nor powers, nor height, nor depth, nor anything else in all creation will be able to separate us from the love of God in Christ Jesus our Lord" (Rom. 8:38). Now *that's* what you call faith: the faith of our fathers, which, as the old hymn says, has endured "in spite of dungeon, fire, and sword."

Virtue #6:
Hope

The Virtue: Hope is the habit of focusing on heaven as the place you hope to go after graduation (not from school— from life in this world!)

The Hurt-You: Despair is the state of mind that gives up hoping in heaven because of a loss of faith that it exists or in the chance to make it there.

Esperanza was sitting on Cloud Nine, feeling fine. All of a sudden, she looked over and saw a messenger angel on a Mercury Grace-o-Line powered motor scooter that looked like it was riding on thin air. Actually, it *was* riding on thin air ... right up to Esperanza's cloud. The messenger angel got off the scooter and said, "The Chief is concerned about your boy, back on earth."

Esperanza looked down but just saw swirling white mists. When she looked back at the messenger, he was getting something a bit like a camcorder out of his Angel's Flight backpack. To her surprise, he put the video camera in front of his face and said, "We're going to do a live feed into his dream, but he'll know it's more than a dream. Just go ahead and start talking to him. He'll hear you. Actually, he'll see you, too."

Esperanza was not sure what was going on. "You mean I need to talk to my son right now?"

"Yes, that's right," the angel said.

"Because he's in trouble?"

"Yes. He thinks nothing's going his way, and he's on the edge of despair."

"What happened to him?

"Well, besides losing you, he lost his job, his girlfriend dumped him, and he's failing his math class."

"Oh, my poor boy. So I can talk to him now?

"Yep, just look here and talk. He'll hear you."

"Okay," she said and paused to gather her thoughts. "Hi, son. I want you to know I'm doing very well. In fact, I'm doing better than I ever did on earth, with all its problems, worries, pain, fears, and uncertainties. Here there is no doubt, no questions, no pain, and nothing that makes us sad. There's only joy, peace, and fulfillment like you wouldn't believe. I can't describe it enough to give you an accurate picture. Some things you can only understand when you get there.

"Anyway, I wanted to tell you not to lose hope. Even when everything seems to turn against you in life, it's only a matter of time before it gets better. It might seem like things won't change, but that's a lie the demonic powers try to suggest to us in our bad times. Have faith in God and his plan for you, and you'll see that life will carry you on to brighter horizons you couldn't have imagined. If you despair and take your own life, you'll never see all the good things God planned for you, and you probably won't make it here where everyone is happy and fulfilled beyond the wildest dreams on earth.

"I know you are sad you lost me, but God had other plans for me. Before I got cancer, I was lost in the aimless pursuit of vanity and pleasures. I'm sorry to say I wasn't always a great mom to you and your sisters. I loved you, but I liked partying with my friends, too. And I didn't think much about God or heaven or the meaning of life. Then I got cancer and all of that changed. As the cancer spread and destroyed my body, in a strange way it healed my soul. I started to really pray to God, to seek forgiveness for my sins, and to develop my relationship with the Church and the sacraments. Remember when I started to take you and your sisters to church every Sunday? In a strange and mysterious way, the cancer brought me back to God. I'm sorry you had to lose me on earth, but it was God's way of saving my soul. I hope you can understand that. And you haven't really lost me; I'm still here pulling and praying for you in heaven. And now I can do that right here in God's presence, even if I can't be directly present to you any more."

Esperanza paused for a moment and looked at the messenger angel, who seemed to wipe his eye. "Angels don't cry," he said, "but sometimes, I just, well, um ..." The angel started some major waterworks. Esperanza thought about her kids on earth and started crying, too. Their tears rolled down and fell into the sky, and, somewhere down on earth, a rainstorm started.

"Okay," said Esperanza, pulling herself together, "let's finish this up." She wiped her eyes, looked into the angelic camcorder, and started talking again. "Listen, my boy: never give up hope. In your darkest moments, remember God always has a plan for you and your life has a purpose, even if you don't know what it is just yet. All you need to do is keep hoping in God, and, in time, his plan for you will be clear. When you get up here with me, you'll see even the worst times of suffering and pain only serve to make you appreciate the joy and fulfillment of heaven even more. Just as a man who has been in the desert really appreciates what it's like to drink water again, so will our suffering, emptiness, and confusion on earth help us appreciate what it's like to be here in heaven, where there is nothing incomplete, no suffering, and no problems. Heaven is filled with the joy and happiness we can never fully experience on earth—the kind that lasts forever and completes our purpose, the kind we were made for.

"Oh, and a couple more things: Cindy was never the right one for you; I told you that a bunch of times even while I was still on earth. But, in a few years, you'll meet the one you were meant for. You can take the math class again in summer school. And they're hiring at Dominic's Pizza, so you can get a new job there, and you'll work hard, do a good job, and really enjoy it. But all these things will only happen if you don't give up hope! I know you'll do the right thing, son, and I believe in you. And God believes in you, even when you may not believe in yourself. Now get back into life, and kick some despair to the curb! Believe, hope, endure, keep your chin up, and never give up. I'll be watching for you and waiting up here. I love you. Good-bye for now, son."

The angel switched off the angelic camcorder, then said, "Oh, no! I had the lens cap on. We're going to need to do the whole thing over!"

"What? Are you crazy?"

The angel laughed. "Just kidding! We got the message into your boy's head. I think it's just what he needed. Once again, the Chief was right; I guess he always is! Thanks, Esperanza!"

What Is Hope?

This story is both an example and an illustration of the virtue of hope. With this virtue, you focus your mind and heart on heaven. Hope is rooted in the virtue of faith, and faith in God leads to the hope of being with him.

What does this mean in the busy, work-a-day world? It means we take time to contemplate God in his angels and his saints, the "multitude which no man could number" (Rev. 7:9), and think of life with God as our life's ultimate goal. It means that even in the darkest, most confusing, and most difficult of times, we never surrender our hope in God and his plan for our lives; this hope can keep us going and help us see a reason for whatever hardship or suffering we may have to endure. It means we have the habit of seeing through all the suffering of our lives and believing there is a reason behind everything and a purpose and plan that will ultimately draw us closer to God. It is this hope that can keep us going and help us retain motivation and a sense of meaning and purpose, no matter how discouraging the situation.

Sometimes, when things turn out exactly opposite what we had wished, our hope in God can help us see that God's plan is making us stronger, better, and wiser. The poet Emily Dickinson once described hope as "the thing with feathers that perches in the soul" and added that it "never stops at all." If you have the virtue of hope, your focus is habitually lifted up beyond this world, and nothing can stop your belief that God's plan for you will work out for the best.

Virtue #7:
Love

The Virtue: Love is the habit of doing good unto others (including God) to the best of one's ability.

The Hurt-Yous: Fear is the state of mind that won't help, won't care, and won't try because you can't afford the risk, might get hurt, or might fail; and hatred is the state of mind that doesn't forgive and usurps the right to judge others, which belongs to God alone.

"Do you really love me?" the girlfriend asked her boyfriend.

"All you need is love," sang the Beatles.

"I love New York," read the bumper sticker.

"We love pizza!" screamed the children.

"Man, I love that song!" said the DJ.

"No one should question that I love my country!" said the politician.

It seems a lot of people use the word *love* for a lot of things these days. To many people, it means a strong feeling of liking or desire. To others it means a commitment or deep sense of loyalty. But what does it mean when Christians refer to the virtue of love?

More Than a Feeling

The virtue of love is much more than a feeling. Bumper stickers symbolize love with a red heart; the heart indicates feelings. But feelings can go up or down: sometimes they may be positive; sometimes they will be negative. You can't really love anyone by trying to feel nice about them. No matter how nice or wonderful other people may be, sooner or later there will be times you won't feel nice or wonderful toward them. What then? For those who define love as nothing more than positive feelings, the only solution is to claim "irreconcilable differences"

(Duh! Any differences are irreconcilable if you don't want to reconcile them) and end the relationship. Real love is much more than feelings: it is a decision of the will.

What does the decision involve? Clearly it means doing good unto others, but what does it mean to do good? There are many ways people define acts of love; probably one of the simplest and easiest to remember is fulfillment of needs. This doesn't mean fulfillment of wants—loving another person doesn't mean trying to do everything he wants you to do. But it does mean you recognize the other person's needs and do your best to fulfill them. This definition of love could also apply to God and the statement in the Bible that "God is love" (1 John 4:8). God is the ultimate fulfillment of all our needs. If we use this definition for love, how do we apply it to God, who is all powerful and has no needs? God has a plan, and you were created to play your part in it. You love God by responding to his call in every moment of your life. "And whatever you do, in word or deed, do everything in the name of the Lord Jesus" (Col. 3:17). You love God by fulfilling the part in his plan that only you can fulfill. You may have no idea what he has in store for you. St. Joan of Arc was a simple peasant girl from a poor family when God called her to lead the army of France and free her country from foreign rule. While his plan for your life is probably not that fantastic, it may still take you beyond your wildest dreams. Or it may be a quiet, humble life, like the kind led by St. Therese of Lisieux; but by loving God, you will have the kind of happiness and fulfillment that never end, both in this life and the next.

Love in the Bible

When Christ was asked about the greatest commandment, he said, "[You]... shall love the Lord your God with all your heart, and with all your soul, and with all your mind, and with all your strength." Then he followed that statement with, "The second is this, 'You shall love your neighbor as yourself'" (Mark 12:30–31). These statements, as well as the Our Father and statements in other parts of the Gospels, make it clear that no one can love God in isolation. Any real love for God will flow out toward others, or it is not real love for God. If we keep the simple definition of love as fulfillment of needs, it's natural for everyone to fulfill their own needs: when your body needs food, you eat; when you need shelter and clothing, you go to your home or get dressed. But to love others as you love yourself means you give the needs of others equal priority to your own needs. And when it lies in your power to fulfill their needs, you do it with the same attitude as if you were fulfilling your own needs.

What does it look like when a Christian has the virtue of love? Probably the best description of this behavior (and one of the most famous) can be found in St. Paul's First Letter to the Corinthians: "Love is patient, love is kind; love is not jealous or boastful; it is not arrogant or rude. Love does not insist on its own way; it is not irritable or resentful; it does not rejoice at wrong, but rejoices in the right. Love bears all things, believes all things, hopes all things, endures all things" (1 Cor. 13:4–7). St. Paul also makes clear that love is the greatest of the virtues: "So faith, hope, and love abide, these three; but the greatest of these is love" (1 Cor. 13:13). All the commandments and teachings of the Law of Moses are fulfilled in the love of God and neighbor.

St. John does not contrast love with hatred, but rather with fear. "There is no fear in love, but perfect love casts out fear. For fear has to do with punishment, and he who fears is not perfected in love" (1 John 4:18). The more you understand and listen to God (who is Love), the less you listen to fear. The more you have true love in your heart, the less power fear (including anxiety, worry, or stress) has over your life and the more you are free to enjoy life and take on the challenges of living a good life in a world "where evil brings profit and virtue none at all" (as the character Don Quixote expressed in the Broadway play *Man of La Mancha*).

Love Is Both Conditional and Unconditional

The contemporary Catholic author and philosopher Mary Rosera Joyce once characterized God's love as having both a masculine and a feminine voice (in her book *Women and Choice*). The feminine voice is unconditional: God loves us for who we are no matter what we do. The masculine voice is conditional: God loves us if we do good and avoid evil. This is found in Christ's statement, "You are my friends if you do what I command you" (John 15:14). In the same way, our love for others should be both unconditional—we love them as children of God no matter how sinful they may be—and conditional—we love them when they do the right thing and don't do the wrong thing. That's what the old saying "to hate the sin but love the sinner" means.

That sounds nice, but how do we do it? Well, the first thing to remember is that love is a decision, not a feeling. To love others as God calls us to requires us to make a choice (again and again, day after day) to wish the best for them and to focus on what is good in them. Thomas Merton wrote that saints become saints not because everybody admires them but because they learn to admire everybody else. All people have some good in them, and by focusing on that we help to multiply it. On the other hand, if we focus on their faults we multiply the negative. When St. Maximilian Kolbe was a young man, he wrote this piece of advice to himself: "Don't worry about evil in others." While there is a time and a place to confront evildoers (conditional love of good actions leads to challenging of bad actions), St. Maximilian recognized that others' faults can be a trap for us, a snare the devils set for us in which we become preoccupied with the bad things that others do and fail to pay attention to the faults we can do something about—our own. Therefore, the important thing to remember about hating a sin but loving a sinner is that once we have attempted to discourage or correct someone else's sin we must let it go and not think about it. Just as you learn to let your own mistakes go and leave your past behind, you need to do the same for the mistakes and faults of others.

Another important thing to remember about love as a decision is this: loving others is not the same as liking others. There will always be people you like and others you don't; our feelings are not acts of our wills, they just happen to us. God's call to love others does not mean we try to manufacture false feelings, even for those who are doing despicable things. Instead, when we see people doing wrong things or trying to harm us or those we love, our natural reaction is dislike. There may even be times when we have to act against others to defend ourselves or our friends or family. But once the fighting is over, what then? Many people who do not understand Christ's teachings carry hatred in their hearts for their enemies. But Christ's way is different. "Love your enemies" (Luke 6:27) means you make the decision to try to fulfill the needs even of those who hate you. Granted, if someone is set on harming you or your loved ones, they may need to be stopped. But if you succeed in stopping them, you don't kick them when they are down. For example, a Christian soldier in a just war who captures an enemy always treats him with mercy. Instead of hating those who hate you, God calls you to rise above them and offer help in their hour of need—to conquer evil with good, or hatred and fear with love. For example, St. Thomas More used to pray for his enemies by asking God to "have mercy on … all that bear me evil will and would me harm, and their faults and mine together."

The Crown of the Virtues

The cardinal virtues prepare us for the theological virtues, and the greatest of the theological virtues is love. All the other virtues, without love, are worthless, as St. Paul pointed out. Even if you don't have all the other virtues, love helps you learn the rest. Anyone can make the decision to love, whether they are rich or poor, young or old, in or out, well educated or a dropout, up or down. Whenever you choose to love, rather than fear or hate, you are taking a step toward God. As St. John put it, "Beloved, let us love one another; for love is of God and he who loves is born of God and knows God. He who does not love does not know God; for God is love" (1 John 4:7–8). And so, step by step, day by day, we choose God by choosing love, which is the heart of the Christian faith.

Afterword: Recommendations for Further Reading

As you have discovered if you read all the preceding pages, there are ten Commandments, eight Beatitudes, and seven Virtues. If it were up to me (even though it's not), there would be one more virtue to add to the list. The eighth virtue would be ... (drum roll, please) ... Good Reading.

Why? Because good reading is necessary to keep the faith in today's world, to grow and develop in goodness, and to remain true to one's calling in a world that throws obstacles, trials, and temptations in one's path. You can learn some things by talking to people. You can learn some things by watching TV, seeing movies, or going on the Internet. You can learn some things in school or by listening to a good homily in church. Some things you only learn by experience. But there are zillions of things you only learn if you read good books. Good reading is a virtue in today's world and is indispensable for anyone who hopes to stay true to their faith.

Note that the phrase is *good reading*. There are a lot of things out there that are definitely not good reading; just as you need to choose your friends wisely, you need to choose your books wisely as well. Probably the best example of a wildly popular novel that all sorts of people have recommended is *The Da Vinci Code,* by Dan Brown. It topped the bestseller list for over a year, but it contains all sorts of lies and misrepresentations about history, the Bible, and the Catholic Church. Was it a commercial success? Absolutely. Is it good reading? No way. There are hundreds of other books far more worthy of your time and attention.

Some of those books and authors are listed here. These are some of the authors and books that can help you persevere in living a good and godly life.

The modern author quoted most in *God Rules* is C. S. Lewis. You've probably read (or at least heard of) his series *The Chronicles of Narnia,* which was written for kids and has been made (and is being made) into a number of movies. What you may not have read yet (but should) are his books for adults. A good starter book—because it's only about 120 pages—is *The Great Divorce*, which offers a fantastic bus ride from hell to heaven featuring all the people you meet along the way. Those who get off the bus and walk toward the light (heaven) call their former location "purgatory," while those who turn around and go back call it "hell." Two other good introductory books are *The Screwtape Letters*—a series of wise and humorous letters from a senior devil to a junior devil on how to win human souls—and *Mere Christianity*, a great defense of the belief in God versus atheism and the Christian faith versus other faiths. I first read these books as a teenager, and they helped form my faith and gave me answers to the attacks against faith found in modern colleges and universities. (Lewis was a former atheist and a professor at Oxford and Cambridge Universities for his adult life.)

The classic literature mentioned in this book is also worth reading, if and when you're up to it. The works of Shakespeare, Milton, Dumas, and Hugo (for example) can all serve to remind us why we should choose good and avoid or fight against evil. But these are works any good teacher or professor would encourage you to read. The recommendations that follow are for authors or books you may not have heard about.

For those who have an interest in psychology with a religious focus, two authors mentioned are highly recommended: Victor Frankl and Conrad Baars. Both were imprisoned for a number of years in Hitler's concentration camps, and both went on to write powerful books that argued for man's spiritual natural. Mainstream psychiatry and psychology are mistaken to treat man as an animal. Frankl argues this case persuasively in his classic book, *Man's Search for Meaning*. Baars also makes a parallel case in his books, two of which are user-friendly for the nonspecialist—*Born Only Once* and *Feeling and Healing Your Emotions* (they are available at www.conradbaars.com).

And for those who would like good, solid materials related to teens and sexuality, there are two highly recommended books that are available from their authors: *Sexual Wisdom,* by Dr. Richard Wetzel, is available through www.sexualwisdom.com, and *Friends: For Teens,* by Mary Rosera Joyce, is available through this address: Lifecom, PO Box 1832, St. Cloud, MN 56302. I would also highly recommend

Joyce's earlier book, *Women and Choice,* for those who enjoy good philosophy; it is a great Catholic response to the women's movement.

Of course, it's hard to do better for strengthening and supporting a virtuous life in a young soul than by reading good biographies of great people. Any book about the lives of the saints published by Ignatius Press or another solid, reputable Catholic publisher is well worth a read. A specific example of a good biography is *Joan of Arc,* by one of the greatest of American authors—Mark Twain. This book not only helps you learn about an amazing young saint, but it also helps you appreciate one of the most important authors of American literature. Mark Twain admired the Catholic saint enough to research her life and write her biography, and his book is still in print. Two biographies about important World War II–era leaders that young people today would find fascinating are *The Myth of Hitler's Pope,* by Rabbi David Dalin, and *Churchill: A Life*, by Martin Gilbert. The book by Dalin explores the heroic actions of Pius XII, who saved the lives of hundreds of thousands of Jews, and explodes all the lies about him from authors with anti-Catholic agendas. Gilbert's book tells the story of Winston S. Churchill, the prime minister of Britain, who defended Christian values and delayed Hitler's conquest of Europe for about two years, until the United States entered the war. In case you would like to learn more about the life of Pope John Paul II, there is only one biography that was requested by John Paul II himself: *Witness to Hope* by George Weigel. It's a job to read (at about 1000 pages), but it helps readers to understand the pope on his own terms, not as filtered through the biases and prejudices of a typical secular humanist journalist (or dissenting Catholic author who thinks and writes like a typical secular humanist journalist).

Several autobiographies are also worth reading: some because they show us about the Catholic faith, some because they teach us about important people and events, and others because they do both. Two great conversion stories are *The Long Loneliness,* by Dorothy Day, and *The Seven Storey Mountain,* by Thomas Merton. Both Day and Merton were brilliant people who made names for themselves as writers and intellectuals; each then gave up many of their former views (and friends) to enter the Catholic Church. Three autobiographies of important world leaders that are both interesting and inspiring are those of Mahatma Gandhi (*My Experiments with Truth*), Anwar Sadat *(In Search of Identity),* and Lech Walesa (*A Way of Hope*). Gandhi is an interesting figure because, as both his autobiography and the film about his life show, he applied the teachings of Christ to a political struggle and brought about the peaceful withdrawal of British rule from India. A few decades later, his style and tactics would be adopted by Dr. Martin Luther King, Jr. to successfully end racial segregation in the United States. The book by Sadat, a former president of Egypt, describes his efforts leading the movement among Arab nations to recognize the state of Israel and become allies of the United States. Finally, the autobiography of Lech Walesa tells the fascinating story of this humble Polish electrician who led the Solidarnosc movement and eventually brought down the Soviet communist empire in 1989. Walesa's story is not only fascinating because of his success in ending communism in Eastern Europe, but it is also inspiring because of the depth and significance of his intensely devout Catholic faith. Both his leadership and the election and leadership of the first Polish Pope in 1978 show how the peaceful defeat of the most bloody, atheistic ideology in history was a great triumph for the Catholic Church.

You may not be up for reading all the books mentioned above, but …

You do need

To read to feed

The seed of creed and deed

That'll surely lead

To the One who did bleed

To feed your need

May our Lord and our Lady, the angels and the saints, bless, protect, and guide you in all you do, today and in all the days that make up the great adventure of the rest of your life. Make it a good one.

Made in the USA
Lexington, KY
24 March 2013